Penguin Monarchs

THE HOUSE OF TUDOR

Henry VII	Sean Cunningham
Henry VIII	John Guy
Edward VI	Stephen Alford
Mary I	John Edwards
Elizabeth I	Helen Castor

THE HOUSE OF STUART

James I	Thomas Cogswell
Charles I	Mark Kishlansky
[Cromwell	David Horspool]
Charles II	Clare Jackson
James II	David Womersley
William III & Mary II	Jonathan Keates
Anne	Richard Hewlings

THE HOUSE OF HANOVER

George I	Tim Blanning
George II	Norman Davies
George III	Amanda Foreman
George IV	Stella Tillyard
William IV	Roger Knight
Victoria	Jane Ridley

THE HOUSES OF SAXE-COBURG & GOTHA AND WINDSOR

Edward VII	Richard Davenport-Hines
George V	David Cannadine
Edward VIII	Piers Brendon
George VI	Philip Ziegler
Elizabeth II	Douglas Hurd

MARC MORRIS

William I

England's Conqueror

ALLEN LANE
an imprint of
PENGUIN BOOKS

ALLEN LANE

UK | USA | Canada | Ireland | Australia
India | New Zealand | South Africa

Penguin Books is part of the Penguin Random House group of companies
whose addresses can be found at global.penguinrandomhouse.com

First published 2016
001

Copyright © Marc Morris, 2016

The moral right of the author has been asserted

Set in 9.5/13.5 pt Sabon LT Std
Typeset by Jouve (UK), Milton Keynes
Printed in Great Britain by Clays Ltd, St Ives plc

ISBN: 978-0-141-97784-3

Contents

To John Gillingham

England and Normandy

N

North Sea

Durham

York • Stamford Bridge

Chester

Lincoln

Nottingham

Stafford

Peterborough

Ely

Huntingdon • Cambridge

Warwick

Gloucester

Oxford • Berkhamsted

Wallingford

London

Cardiff

Colchester

Sandwich

Canterbury • Dover

Old Sarum • Winchester

Battle • Hastings

Bosham

Pevensey

Isle of Wight

English Channel

Montreuil

St Valéry

Arques

Mortemer

Gerberoy

Dives

Bec • Rouen

Bayeux • Caen

Varaville

Vaudreuil

Val-ès-Dunes

Évreux • Mantes

Falaise

Paris

Tillières

Thimert

Dol • Domfront

Alençon

Ambrières

100 miles

100 km

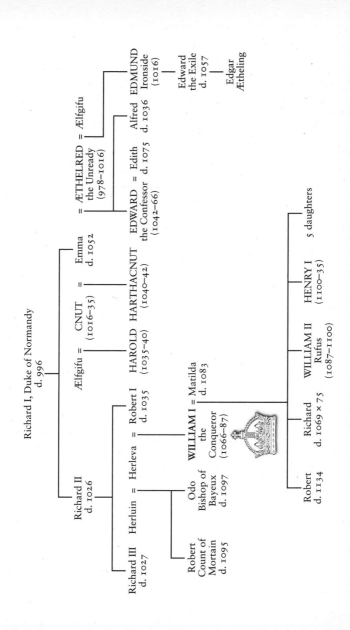

William I

I
Introduction

The monks of Westminster had started the year by burying a king, and now they were ending it by enthroning a new one.

The dead king, Edward the Confessor, had been the monks' dearest friend. During his long reign he had transformed the site of their abbey, a small island in the Thames to the west of London, into a seat of royal power, establishing a palace there for himself and rebuilding the ancient monastery, or minster, on a grand scale. The new church was a magnificent affair, the largest in Britain, and built in a strikingly novel 'Romanesque' style. It had been only recently consecrated, and was still not quite finished, at the time of the old king's death on 5 January 1066. The following day the monks had reverentially laid him to rest in front of its high altar.

Now, almost twelve months later, they were preparing for the coronation of William, Duke of Normandy – though Englishmen sometimes referred to him by a different name. William was Edward's second cousin and, according to some, his nominated successor. But the duke's claim to the throne had been bitterly contested. The Confessor had been replaced in the first instance by his

brother-in-law, Harold Godwineson, the most powerful
earl in England and a candidate with strong popular backing. The result had been the most famous succession
dispute in English history. After months of anxious waiting and preparation, William had invaded that autumn
and fought Harold at the Battle of Hastings, killing his
rival and many thousands of others. A few weeks later the
surviving English in London had submitted and begged
him to take the crown.

And so, on Christmas Day 1066, the Duke of Normandy
entered the pristine abbey church at Westminster for his
coronation ceremony. He was nearly forty years old, and
this was the climactic moment of his life – the sacred ritual
that would transform him from a duke into a king, and
herald the beginning of what he hoped would be a long,
glorious and peaceful reign. His English subjects, too,
were hopeful that William's rule would bring peace and
security, for in recent months they had experienced little
besides death and destruction. Before the crown was
placed on his head, the new king swore to govern his kingdom according to the best customs of his predecessors.

But no sooner had this promise been made than the
prospect of a better future was shattered. At some point
during the proceedings, the audience was asked whether
they would accept William as their new ruler, and
responded with a shout of acclamation. This was custom-
ary behaviour for an English coronation, but the Norman
soldiers who had been left outside to guard the church,
hearing a clamour of foreign voices from within, assumed
that treachery was afoot, and began setting fire to the

surrounding buildings – such at least is the excuse for their behaviour tendered by the Norman chronicler who first recounted the tale. When those inside realized that the rest of Westminster was ablaze, they rushed from the abbey in all directions, some to fight the flames, others to indulge in opportunistic looting. Only the clergy who were performing the service remained inside, and completed the ceremony in terror. William himself, we are told, was left trembling from head to foot. At the very moment God had been called upon to bless his rule, all around were scenes of chaos and destruction.[1]

To chroniclers who wrote with the benefit of hindsight, this was an omen of the catastrophes to come. William's reign did indeed prove to be long, but it was far from peaceful. While he wore the crown, England experienced greater and more seismic change than at any point before or since. The years immediately after his coronation were ones of almost constant violence, filled with English rebellion, Norman repression and even Viking invasion. Huge areas of the country were laid waste with fire and sword, especially the North, which was harried into submission without mercy during the winter of 1069–70. The old ruling elite of England were swept away in their thousands and replaced by continental newcomers, who spoke a different language and had very different views about the way society should be ordered. Hundreds of castles were constructed all over the kingdom to enforce Norman rule, and every major abbey and cathedral was ripped down and rebuilt. The tenurial map of England was torn up and radically redrawn, giving greater power than ever before to the king. At the end of his career, when William attempted to assess the scale of this transformation by launching a great survey, his subjects compared it to the Last Judgement of God.

Thanks to the Domesday Book, we know more about eleventh-century England than any other medieval society anywhere in the world. Accurate information about William himself, by contrast, is comparatively scarce. Domesday apart, the administrative sources for his reign are lacking, and royal letters and charters survive only where they have been kept in cathedral archives or copied into monastic cartularies. The deficit of such documents means that recovering even basic facts about William's career is difficult. Most of the time we cannot say where he was or who he was with from one month to the next, and in some cases whole years of his life, even after his accession as King of England, are effectively blank. Such letters and charters as do survive, moreover, are formal affairs, not windows into William's personality. The kind of private correspondence that sometimes illuminates the inner thoughts of later English monarchs simply does not exist.

This means that the only way we can approach William's character and actions is through the words of those who described them at the time – monks or clerics who wrote chronicles and histories of the period. Some of these accounts can be extremely detailed, offering credible information about William's activities and plausible interpretations of his motives. And yet, at the same time, their testimony has to be used with caution. Some chroniclers, such as the king's chaplain, William of Poitiers, were writing what we would regard as propaganda, and were concerned at all times with presenting him in the best possible light. All chroniclers, being churchmen, tended to interpret events as the workings of God's will, and in many cases wrote their histories for the moral edification of their readers rather than to preserve a strictly accurate record of the past. The anonymous English monk who wrote William's obituary in the *Anglo-Saxon Chronicle* – one of our most valuable sources – explained that he had set down both the good and evil things about the king 'so that people may cherish the good and utterly eschew the evil, and follow the path that leads to the kingdom of heaven'. Another outstandingly important chronicler, Orderic Vitalis, was fond of putting words into the mouths of the individuals he was writing about. 'O my friends,' says William on his deathbed, 'I am weighed down with the burden of my sins, and tremble, for I must soon face the terrible judgement of God.' The dying king then goes on to deliver a seven-page last speech, in which he reviews his whole career but gets many of the details wrong, including his own age. 'I treated the native inhabitants of the kingdom with unreasonable severity, cruelly oppressed high and low, unjustly disinherited many and caused the death of thousands by starvation and war.' It is important to remember that Orderic was born in England, and that these are his words, not William's.[2]

A final frustration is that we have almost no clues about what William looked like. The images of his face that appear on English coins are highly stylized representations, not attempts at portraiture, and the well-known depictions of him on the Bayeux Tapestry tell us little beyond the fact that he apparently sported the same close-cropped hairstyle as every other eleventh-century Norman knight. His tomb in Caen, typically for its time, was not topped with an effigy, only an inscribed stone slab. When it was opened in 1522 on the orders of the pope, observers reported that William's skeleton was large and long-limbed, but their conclusions are difficult to verify because the tomb was destroyed forty years later when the abbey was desecrated by French Protestants. All that was salvaged from the wreckage was a single thigh bone, which has since been reburied and exhumed several times. Archaeologists and anthropologists who examined it in 1987 estimated that the king's overall height was about 173 cm (5 feet 8 inches). Assuming the bone really did belong to William, therefore, his height was only a little above the average for a medieval adult male (about 170 cm), and he was only 4 cm taller than his great-great-grandson, King John, whom contemporaries regarded as short. According to the chronicler William of Malmesbury, writing in the 1120s, William was immensely stout and strong, able to draw a bow that others could not bend while spurring his horse to a gallop, and so ferocious that his roared oaths would terrify those around him.[3]

How was it, then, that this extraordinary man, who changed England more than any other, came to be crowned on Christmas Day 1066?

2
The Bastard

It was also at Christmas, thirty-two years earlier, that another duke of Normandy startled his great men by announcing his intention to visit Jerusalem. Duke Robert, known to posterity as both 'the Magnificent' and 'the Devil', had come to power seven years previously, following the sudden death of his older brother, Richard, and malicious tongues would later whisper that he wanted to go on pilgrimage to the Holy Land because he had been responsible for this brother's murder. At the time, however, the magnates of Normandy were more concerned about what would happen if he failed to return from his proposed adventure, for a trip to the Middle East in the Middle Ages was a perilous undertaking, and the duke had neither brothers nor sons to succeed him.

At least, not legitimate ones. But some years earlier, around the time of his accession or shortly before, Robert had enjoyed a brief encounter with a girl from the town of Falaise in central Normandy. Her name was Herleva, and she was the daughter of Fulbert, variously identified in the sources as a ducal chamberlain, a tanner and an under-taker. According to later legend, she had caught the duke's eye from afar, either while dancing or washing her clothes in the river. However it came to pass, Herleva in due course gave birth to a son whom Robert recognized and raised with sufficient honour. In order to mollify his anxious magnates at Christmas 1034, the duke presented them with this seven-year-old boy and made them swear an oath to accept him as their future ruler.

It was a prudent move because, as feared, Robert never returned from his pious expedition. He made it as far as Jerusalem and reportedly wept for a week at Christ's tomb, but fell sick on his homeward journey and died on 2 July 1035 at Nicaea, where he was buried by his own men. It would have taken at least two months for the news to reach Normandy, at which point the rule of his young heir, the future William the Conqueror, began.[1]

Some people were evidently scandalized at the accession of a child who had not been conceived within the bounds of holy matrimony. In another part of France, the Burgundian chronicler Ralph Glaber wrote that Robert's lack of a legitimate son had been a cause of great distress to his people, and suggested that some thought it abominable that the duke had been succeeded by a bastard. In the same breath, however, Glaber conceded that the dukes of Normandy had always been happy to honour the offspring of their concubines and accept them as their heirs. 'This had been the custom of this people', the chronicler admitted, 'ever since they first appeared in Gaul.'[2]

The Normans had first arrived in Gaul (the former Roman province roughly equivalent to modern France) in the ninth century as Viking raiders – their name, given to them by their enemies, signified 'men of the North'.

Around the start of the tenth century some of them started to settle in the area around Rouen and colonized the ancient Roman region of Neustria, so that over time it came to be known by the new name of 'Normandy'. In the century that followed they ditched most of their Viking ways and adopted the manners and customs of their new neighbours, learning to speak French, giving their children French names, embracing Christianity, and refounding some of the churches and monasteries that their not-too-distant ancestors had looted and destroyed. And yet, as Ralph Glaber's comment shows, people who lived in other parts of France still felt that the Normans had some distance to travel before they could be regarded as fully civilized.

If William's bastardy was not an immediate problem in 1035, his youth most certainly was. A boy of seven or eight could not rule in his own right, and while he grew to manhood the necessary leadership would have to be provided by others. In the first instance Normandy was governed by his great-uncle, Archbishop Robert of Rouen, who managed to keep order until his death in 1037, but after that chaos ensued as local lords began usurping ducal authority and taking power into their own hands. Castles, which had started to appear in western Europe around the turn of the first millennium, suddenly began to sprout up across Normandy in great numbers. Compared to later examples they were for the most part crudely built affairs of earth and timber, but nonetheless brutally effective for men who wished to dominate their surroundings and defend their lands from the attacks of neighbours. 'Having dared to establish themselves securely in their own fortifications,' wrote the contemporary chronicler William of Jumièges, 'they immediately hatched plots and rebellions, and fierce fires were lit all over the country.'

Several of these plots involved gaining control of the young duke. William's father had taken the precaution of naming several guardians for his son, but one by one they were assassinated. Count Alan of Brittany and Count Gilbert of Brionne were killed in the autumn of 1040, and the boy's tutor, Turold, was murdered in 1041. Osbern, who was steward of the ducal household, had his throat cut in Vaudreuil Castle as he slept in the same room as William. Those behind this spate of killings evidently succeeded in their aim of taking over Normandy's government. William of Jumièges refrained from naming them, because 'they are the very men who now surround the duke'.[3]

The only hope of ending these bloody feuds and restoring order was for William to assert his personal authority. Not long after the above atrocities, when he was about fifteen years old, the young duke was knighted, signifying that he had come of age and was ready to wield power in his own right. For his chaplain, William of Poitiers, this was a watershed moment, 'a most joyful day' for those who desired 'peace and justice'. Poitiers had been a knight himself before turning to the priesthood, and his biography of William is our most valuable source for the duke's career. As a sometime member of the ducal household he is, of course, extremely biased in his master's favour. News of William's knighting, we are assured, 'spread fear throughout France; Gaul had not another man who was reputed to be such a knight in arms'. But Poitiers, who may have heard William's confession, takes us closer into the presence of the Conqueror than any other writer.

Poitiers may be exaggerating, but there are other signs that William's assumption of authority began to have an effect. The documents the duke issued in the mid 1040s show he was surrounding himself with his own supporters – men of a similar age who would continue to serve him loyally for the rest of their lives. At the same time, says Poitiers, William began 'forcefully demanding' the services owed to him by others – in other words, seeking to claw back some of the power that had been lost during his long minority.[4]

Unsurprisingly, the lords who had done well during the time of self-help reacted badly to the duke's demands, and sought to replace him with his legitimate cousin, Guy of Brionne. Towards the end of 1046 the counts and viscounts of western Normandy rose in what was clearly a very serious rebellion. William, who was apparently staying in that part of the duchy when news of the conspiracy broke, had to race for his life to the safety of his birthplace at Falaise, and then fled from Normandy altogether to seek help from the King of France.

The French king, Henry I, was nothing like as powerful as his august title implies. During the tenth century, partly as a result of invasions like the Norman takeover of Neustria, royal authority in France had fragmented, and the kings themselves were reduced to ruling only a small patch of territory centred on their capital at Paris. 'Although first among the Franks,' the Bishop of Laon had said to Henry's father, Robert II, 'you are but a serf in the order of kings.'

Diminished as he was compared to his ancestors, the French king remained a substantial player in the fractious politics of northern France, and the dukes of Normandy had always taken care to maintain cordial relations by acknowledging royal authority, however token it might be in reality. Henry I had approved Duke Robert's plan for William to succeed him in 1035, and had also knighted the boy-duke a few years later, almost certainly receiving an oath of loyalty in return. In his hour of need, therefore, William looked to the French king for military aid.

Henry fulfilled his side of the bargain by raising an army, and at the start of 1047 the two men rode to confront the duke's enemies. They met them at a place in central Normandy called Val-ès-Dunes, and a bloody battle ensued. In the annals of military history it was not especially noteworthy – few reliable details have come down to us, and not even the date is known – but in terms of William's career it was decisive. That day the young duke crushed his domestic opponents and put paid once and for all to their plan to replace him. In the wake of his victory he was able to seize and destroy their castles, and redistribute their lands to those who had remained loyal. After a lengthy siege of his castle at Brionne the rebellion's figurehead, Count Guy, was driven into exile. Val-ès-Dunes, declared William of Jumièges, was a 'happy battle, that in one day ruined so many castles of criminals and houses of evil-doers'.[5]

There remained one more task for William to fulfil in order to restore stability to his duchy. 'Now that the duke, flourishing in his youthful strength, was passed the age of adolescence,' explains Jumièges, 'his magnates urgently drew attention to the problem of his offspring and the succession.' If he was to deter future pretenders like Count Guy from eyeing his position, it was essential for William to get married and start producing sons. After talking the matter over with his advisers, he decided to set his cap at Matilda, a daughter of Baldwin, Count of Flanders. An alliance with Flanders would have the additional advantage of establishing good relations with a powerful neighbour, and as for Matilda herself, she was a few years younger than William and reportedly 'very beautiful'. Her tomb in Caen, like his, was sacked in the sixteenth century, but enough of her skeleton survived for modern archaeologists to estimate her height as 152 cm, or 5 feet (not 4 feet 2 inches, as is still sometimes erroneously asserted). The only problem at first was the pope, who vetoed the marriage in the autumn of 1049, claiming that the couple were too closely related. The real reason for his objection was probably his own bad relations with Count Baldwin, and it seems that this obstacle was quickly overcome. At some point before 1051 the count escorted his daughter to Normandy and she and William were married in Rouen amid scenes of great rejoicing.[6]

The young duke, now in his early twenties, had already achieved a great deal. He had survived a dangerous and traumatic childhood, defeated his enemies in battle and made an advantageous marriage to a beautiful young woman. It was at this point that his story took an interesting twist, when he received an invitation to visit the King of England.

3
The Pledge

In 1051 Edward the Confessor had confounded the expectations of those who had written him off as a pious nonentity. Since his accession to the English throne nine years earlier the king had done almost nothing without first obtaining the nod of his powerful father-in-law, Earl Godwine, but that autumn he had stood up to the earl and driven him into exile. 'If any Englishman had been told that events would take this turn, he would have been very surprised,' admitted the anonymous author of the *Anglo-Saxon Chronicle*, 'for Godwine had risen to such great eminence as if he ruled the king and all England.'[1]

If life had taught Edward anything, however, it was how to bide his time. When he was born, almost fifty years earlier, England was in the grip of an ongoing crisis. The country had been created during the previous century from several smaller Anglo-Saxon kingdoms, such as Mercia, East Anglia and Northumbria; Edward's ancestors, the kings of Wessex, had forged them together in the process of driving out an earlier wave of Viking settlers. But as the century had drawn to a close the Vikings had returned in greater numbers, and by the time of Edward's birth they were raiding and destroying wherever they pleased. His father, the hapless Æthelred the Unready, proved unequal to the task of resisting them, and died in 1016 in the midst of a full-scale Danish invasion. By the end of that year the throne had passed to the all-conquering King Cnut, a ruler with a reputation for dealing mercilessly with his opponents. Edward, by this point in his early teens, fled across the Channel, and eventually ended up in Normandy.

Normandy was an obvious place for Edward to seek refuge, for he was himself half Norman. In 1002 his father had taken Emma, the sister of Duke Richard II of Normandy, as his second wife. Emma's Norman roots meant that her children (Edward and his younger siblings Alfred and Godgifu) were welcomed at her brother's court, but she saw to her own safety by quite different means, marrying her late husband's supplanter, King Cnut, and thereby becoming Queen of England for a second time, but abandoning her children in the process.[2]

In 1016, therefore, Edward's fortunes were at their lowest ebb, and his future prospects seemed less than glittering. Effectively orphaned, for the next twenty-five years he remained at the court of his Norman kinsmen, treated honourably but apparently receiving nothing in the way of lands or titles. On two occasions in the 1030s he attempted to return to England with Norman military support, but both expeditions ended in failure. When Cnut died in 1035 he was succeeded by his own sons, first Harold, who reigned until his death in 1040, and then Harthacnut.

It was at this point that Edward's fortunes took a surprising upward turn, for Harthacnut proved to be a highly unpopular king, who imposed swingeing taxes and harried his subjects when they refused to pay up. Barely a year after his succession his nobles appear to have turned against him and forced him into an extraordinary power-sharing arrangement. In 1041 Edward was summoned from Normandy and sworn in as Harthacnut's co-ruler. When the unpopular Dane collapsed and died at a wedding feast the following year, Edward was unanimously chosen as the country's new king. It was an astonishingly swift turnaround for a man who had spent a quarter of a century in apparently hopeless foreign exile. Against all expectations, the Danish royal house had failed and the ancient line of Wessex had been restored.

But Edward had one outstanding problem. His return to England had been brokered by the kingdom's most powerful magnate, Earl Godwine of Wessex, who expected in return to have a dominant role in government. The new king, however, harboured a deep-seated hatred of the earl, holding him responsible for a heinous crime. In 1036, around the time of Edward's second unsuccessful attempt to reclaim England by force, his younger brother Alfred had made a similar bid for power, landing on the south coast with a small band of followers. Shortly after their arrival they were met by Godwine, who received them warmly and entertained them for the evening, but then betrayed them. Alfred's followers were variously murdered, mutilated and sold into slavery, and Alfred himself died a short time later after being deliberately blinded.[3]

After Edward's accession Godwine attempted to bury the hatchet, swearing he had not wished to harm Alfred and plying the king with gifts, including a fully crewed, elaborately gilded warship. Edward initially had no choice but to play along. At the start of his reign he was a stranger in a strange land, and his habits, manners and associates were French. His English was probably rusty and he had few genuine friends in England. He needed Godwine's support to survive, and therefore had to fall in with the earl's wishes. In the early 1040s two of Godwine's sons and one of his nephews were promoted to the rank of earl, and in 1045 the king himself was married to Godwine's daughter, Edith.

But towards the end of the same decade, tension between the two men began to mount. They fell out over foreign policy when Edward rejected Godwine's suggestion of sending military aid to the embattled King of Denmark. They also disagreed over Church appointments, as Edward began advancing his own candidates to bishoprics and abbacies as they fell vacant. In 1051 the king insisted on appointing his Norman friend and long-time counsellor, Robert of Jumièges, as the new Archbishop of Canterbury, in the face of opposition from the monks of Canterbury, who favoured one of their own number, who also happened to be one of Godwine's kinsmen. In June that year Jumièges refused to consecrate the earl's candidate for the bishopric of London, and accused him of invading Canterbury's lands. The final straw came at the end of August, when Edward received a visit from his brother-in-law, the Count of Boulogne. On their way home the count and his men clashed with the citizens of Dover with the result that many on both sides were killed. After listening to his brother-in-law's complaint the king decided to punish

Dover, and ordered Godwine, the local earl, to attack the town. Godwine refused, declaring that he would not harm his own people.

The earl's open defiance provoked an armed showdown. Godwine and his sons mustered their forces, confident that they could overawe the king. But Edward had been building support elsewhere, and the Earls of Mercia and Northumbria now rallied to his aid. The two sides came close to engaging in Gloucestershire, but at the last moment the commanders in both camps drew back, fearful that civil war would leave them once again exposed to Viking invasion. In the days that followed, however, Edward's army grew and Godwine's men began to desert him. It soon became clear that the king held the whip hand. According to one source, he told the earl he could have peace 'when he gave him back his brother alive'. Realizing that his position was hopeless, Godwine fled overseas with his wife and sons. His daughter, Queen Edith, was banished to a nunnery.[4]

It was at this juncture, immediately after his victory over Godwine, that Edward invited his young second cousin, the Duke of Normandy, to visit him in England. Having described the flight of the Godwines and the banishment of the queen, a well-informed version of the *Anglo-Saxon Chronicle* immediately adds:

> Then soon came Duke William from beyond the sea with a great retinue of Frenchmen, and the king received him and as many of his companions as it pleased him, and let him go again.

Why had Edward summoned William? The *Chronicle* is not very forthcoming, perhaps even reluctant to tell us. All it seems to say is that the duke came to England with a great number of followers, received an audience with the king and then returned home. Norman chroniclers, however, supply a plausible explanation. According to William of Poitiers and William of Jumièges, it was in 1051 that Edward promised his young kinsman the succession to the English throne. These sources are somewhat problematic, in that they were written (or in Jumièges's case, revised) after the Conquest, but in general they command credence. They assert, for example, that the offer of the succession was first carried to William by Edward's chief adviser, Robert of Jumièges, a statement that draws credibility from the fact that Robert did indeed cross the Channel in 1051 in order to travel to Rome to be invested as Archbishop of Canterbury by the pope. This in turn raises the possibility that the issue of the succession had been discussed at Edward's court as early as March that year, when Robert was appointed to his new role. If so, it would add a larger, more potent explanation of the king's clash with Godwine. Since the marriage of his daughter to Edward in 1045, the earl, along with other Englishmen, had been waiting hopefully for the birth of an heir. A son or sons would remove the uncertainty that had plagued England in recent years, and, in Godwine's case, guarantee the security of his own dynasty. But despite the fervent prayers that were offered up, no children, male or female, had appeared. Modern historians tend to posit infertility as the likeliest cause, but contemporaries believed it was because the marriage was never consummated. A source commissioned by the queen herself, *The Life of King Edward*, insisted that Edward was sworn to celibacy.[5]

Down to 1051, therefore, Godwine might still have hoped for a royal grandson. But if Edward made known his intention to pass the throne to William, that hope would have been replaced by fear and anger. Frustrating as the earl must have found relations with the new Norman Archbishop of Canterbury, this was hardly a reason to raise an army and make war on the king. If, on the other hand, the succession was at stake, and with it the Godwine family's grip on power, then the case for armed resistance became more compelling.

Edward's determination to spite Godwine is hardly surprising, given the earl's responsibility for the murder of his brother. Why, though, should he want to bequeath his kingdom to William? Here again the most convincing answer is the one given by the Norman chroniclers: gratitude. William of Poitiers, it is true, exaggerates his case by claiming that Duke William was instrumental in persuading the English to accept Edward's return in 1041. At that time the duke was no more than fourteen years old and disorder in Normandy was at its height. But there can be no real doubt that Edward felt a genuine debt to his Norman cousins, who had taken him in as an exile and brought him up honourably at their court. William may have been too young and powerless to have provided any support before 1041, but his father, Duke Robert, had helped Edward assemble a fleet to invade England in the early 1030s, and William's regents had done the same in 1036.

We do not have to indulge in too much psychological guesswork to see where Edward's true affections lay. As a child he had seen his father and elder brothers die fighting against a Danish invader. His mother had abandoned him in order to marry that invader and become Cnut's queen. His father-in-law had collaborated with Cnut to become the Danish king's right-hand man, and had murdered Edward's only remaining brother. It should hardly surprise us that, when he thought about the succession, the child-less king should want to thwart his Anglo-Danish in-laws and advance the fortunes of the family that had sheltered and raised him.[6]

There was another reason why Edward would have wished to favour William in 1051. At some point during the previous year the young duke had married the daughter of the Count of Flanders, and England's relationship with Flanders was terrible. Throughout the 1040s the count had repeatedly provided safe haven for Edward's enemies, including Anglo-Danes the king had driven into exile and Danish pirates who had raided the English coast. Edward had retaliated in 1049 by sending his fleet to blockade Flemish ports and, predictably enough, it was to the court of the Count of Flanders that Godwine and his family had fled. A marriage alliance between Flanders and Normandy was therefore a deeply disturbing development, since it raised the possibility of a Channel coast hostile from one end to the other.[7]

Edward's intention in inviting William to England in the autumn of 1051 was, therefore, probably twofold. He may have wanted to reaffirm in person the promise of the

English throne made earlier in the year, but he also wanted to bind the duke more closely to him. Here the *Anglo-Saxon Chronicle*'s remark that the king 'received' William and some of his followers is crucial, for the Old English word *underfeng* means 'received as a vassal'. That autumn, the duke knelt before Edward and acknowledged him as his lord.[8]

Alas for Edward, his bid for independence quickly unravelled. The following year Godwine and his family made a concerted effort to reassert themselves. The earl raised a fleet in Flanders, and his sons did the same in Ireland. Late in the summer of 1052 they began raiding the south coast of England, seizing men and ships and rallying others to their cause, which had grown more popular during their exile, perhaps because news of Edward's scheme for a Norman succession had spread. The king certainly saw support for his own position weakening and, having recently taken the decision to disband his mercenary fleet, found he could not muster enough forces to resist his enemies' return. In September Godwine sailed his massive armada up the Thames into London and surrounded Edward's remaining supporters. Powerless to resist, the broken king was obliged to restore the earl and his sons to their earldoms, and to readmit Godwine's daughter to the royal bedchamber. Realizing all was lost, Edward's Norman friends, including Robert of Jumièges, rode hard for the coast and sailed for Normandy, where they doubtless told the duke that any hopes he had entertained about becoming King of England were now utterly forlorn.[9]

4
Bad Neighbours

Although William's visit to England cannot be dated precisely, it is likely to have occurred soon after he scored a significant victory over his troublesome neighbour, Geoffrey of Anjou. Geoffrey had nicknamed himself 'Martel', meaning 'the Hammer', and had been bashing his opponents with considerable success even before his accession as Count of Anjou in 1040. William of Poitiers, despite deploring him as an enemy of the Normans, described Geoffrey as 'remarkably skilled and experienced in the arts of war'. His preferred technique for besting his opponents was to take them prisoner and hold them in custody until they agreed to his territorial demands.[1]

William had first come into conflict with Geoffrey towards the end of the 1040s, when the King of France assembled a coalition of the count's disgruntled neighbours and led an invasion of Anjou. The dukes of Normandy had always supported the French crown when summoned to do so, and William, being heavily in Henry I's debt since Val-ès-Dunes, had shown no hesitation in joining the expedition. According to Poitiers he led the largest contingent, and the king looked to him as his favourite and most valuable counsellor. Henry's only reproach against William at this time, we're told, was that he exposed himself to too much risk in searching for combat. Poitiers goes on to describe an occasion when the young duke, having slipped away from the main host with only four companions, suddenly encountered fifteen enemy knights. Undeterred by the odds, he unhorsed one of his opponents with his lance, and then rode off in pursuit of the others. By the time his companions caught up with him, William had taken seven of the fugitives prisoner. After this, says Poitiers, even Geoffrey Martel would tell people that there was 'no knight or warrior under the sun equal to the count of the Normans'.[2]

Despite William's personal heroics, the invasion of Anjou failed to halt Geoffrey's aggressive expansionism. For several years he had been seeking to extend his power northwards into the county of Maine, and in the spring of 1051, after the death of Maine's existing count, he succeeded. Worse still, from William's point of view, Geoffrey also invaded Normandy, to the extent that he received the submission of Alençon, a town that lay close to Maine in the south of the duchy. In retaliation the duke besieged the town of Domfront, situated on the opposite side of the border in Maine itself, and then led a rapid assault on Alençon, marching through the night in order to surprise its defenders. On arrival he was greeted by the garrison of a small fortress which lay outside the walls, who shouted insults at him, mocking the fact that his mother's family had been undertakers. William responded by quickly taking the fortress and ordering the mutilation of his detractors, thirty-two of whom had their hands and feet lopped off.

The people of Alençon, after witnessing this grisly spectacle, decided to submit. So too, when they heard the news, did the defenders of Domfront.[3]

It is very likely that this clash with Geoffrey Martel was over by the autumn of 1051, enabling William to cross the Channel and visit Edward the Confessor before the year's end. But just as Edward's *annus mirabilis* quickly unravelled, so William experienced a sudden reversal of fortune when the King of France turned against him. This was a major blow, for the dukes of Normandy had maintained friendly relations with their nominal royal overlords for more than century. No contemporary offers a full explanation for this seismic shift, but the fact that it took place immediately after William's visit to England is highly suggestive. As the *Anglo-Saxon Chronicle* tells us, the duke had become Edward's vassal and acknowledged the English king as his lord. That by itself may have been enough to offend Henry, to whom he had already done homage. If Edward also promised William the English succession at this point, there was even more reason for Henry to be displeased. From a French point of view, Normandy was powerful enough as it was. If its duke were also to become King of England, it would make him the most powerful man in France, far greater than the French king himself. William of Poitiers, although he makes no mention of England, explains that Henry was affronted because William was 'neither his friend nor his vassal', and that Normandy, 'which had been under the kings of France from the earliest times, had now been raised almost to a kingdom'.[4]

Henry gave vent to his new-found anger in the first

instance by promoting a rebellion within Normandy – a
revolt led, as in 1047, by a discontented member of the
ducal house. The rebel on this occasion was William,
Count of Arques, a son of Duke Richard II by a second
marriage (and thus half-uncle to the young duke). We can
see from the count's witnessing of ducal charters that he
had been closely involved in government during William's
minority, but the decline in frequency of his attestations
thereafter suggests that he was subsequently edged out.
According to William of Poitiers, the tipping point came
when the count abandoned his nephew's army during the
siege of Domfront, a desertion which the duke punished by
confiscating the mighty castle his uncle had built at Arques.
Some time later, probably in the first half of 1053, the
count re-entered the castle by bribing its guards and began
stocking it ready for war. When William learned that
rebellion was being prepared he rushed to suppress it,
ignoring warnings that all of Upper Normandy had turned
against him, and succeeded in driving the count and his
men inside the castle walls. Since the walls of Arques were
too difficult to breach, William constructed a siege-castle
nearby to stop supplies reaching the rebels, hoping that
hunger would persuade them to surrender.[5]

In the autumn of 1053 Henry I intervened in person,
invading Upper Normandy with the intention of raising
the siege. The garrison William had left in the siege-castle
acquitted themselves well, killing and capturing some of
the French knights in a skirmish, and eventually forcing
the king to retire. Nevertheless, some fresh troops and supplies found their way into Arques, and it was not until the

duke returned to direct the siege himself that the rebels were finally reduced to submission.

No sooner had the fortress fallen, however, than the King of France returned at the head of a far larger host. Smarting at his defeat during the autumn, Henry invaded Normandy early in the new year of 1054 leading a coalition of France's other regional rulers, including the Counts of Aquitaine and Blois, as well as the Count of Anjou, Geoffrey Martel. Their target, according to William of Poitiers, was the Norman capital, Rouen, and their intention was to drive William into exile and reduce his duchy to a desert.[6]

The duke's response, the chronicler continues, was naturally to defend his people by confronting the invaders, but he also explains that William stopped short of engaging Henry in battle 'out of respect for his former friendship and the royal dignity'. The truth was almost certainly that neither side wanted a direct confrontation. Even in the Middle Ages battles were rare events, because their outcomes were highly unpredictable. In the confusion of battle you might end up killing your opponent, but equally you might end up being killed yourself. Most of the time commanders were unwilling to take such a huge risk, and preferred the easier route of devastating their enemies' territory, burning the countryside and destroying towns and villages. According to the less sycophantic William of Jumièges, the duke's tactic in 1054 was to shadow the king's army, attacking any members of it he was able to catch. For a defender, it was safer to wait until an invading army started to run low on food, because the necessity of foraging for fresh supplies would render them vulnerable.[7]

This was how the Normans gained the upper hand in 1054. While William was following Henry's main host in south-eastern Normandy, another group of Normans was shadowing a second French force that had invaded the north-east of the duchy, under the command of the king's brother, Odo. These French troops had barely crossed the border before they dropped their guard and began ravaging and pillaging around the town of Mortemer. The Normans ambushed them at dawn, and by midday those who had not been killed or captured were driven into flight. The news that his brother had been defeated reached the French king later that evening, and persuaded him to withdraw from Normandy the following day.

The collapse of his invasion soon induced Henry to make peace. In return for the release of the French knights taken prisoner at Mortemer, the king agreed to drop his alliance with Geoffrey Martel and promised to recognize any future territorial gains that William might make against the count. A month or so later the duke led an army into Maine and began building a new castle at Ambrières, fifteen miles south of Domfront. Martel attempted to stop its construction, but without success.[8]

As well as expanding his borders, William seized the opportunity to embark on a house-clearing exercise within Normandy. The chief victim was the leader of the 1053 revolt, the Count of Arques, who lost his lands and his castle and was banished into exile. Another major casualty was the count's brother, Mauger, who had been Archbishop of Rouen since 1037. Precisely what role if any Mauger had played in the rebellion is impossible to say, but

William clearly felt he was culpable. A special Church council was convened in the spring of 1054. The archbishop was deposed and sent to live out his remaining days on Guernsey.[9]

The peace that Normandy enjoyed in the mid 1050s did not last long. By the start of 1057 Henry I and Geoffrey Martel were back in each other's company, and in August that year they launched another determined invasion. William of Poitiers claims that their combined forces were not as large as before, but they nevertheless drove deeper into the duchy, ravaging from the southern border to the north coast. Once again, however, they were caught unawares, this time by William himself, who attacked the rearguard of the French army as it was fording the River Dives near the town of Varaville. With many of their men captured, killed or drowned, the invaders withdrew.[10]

On this occasion there were no subsequent peace talks, and hostilities continued. In 1058 William recovered a castle at Tillières that had been lost during his minority to the French king, and captured Henry's own castle at Thimert. What finally put paid to the duke's struggle against both the King of France and the Count of Anjou was their sudden deaths within a few months of each other in 1060. Henry died in August after taking some medicine and ignoring his doctor's orders not to drink, Geoffrey in November from an unknown illness, reportedly in great pain. Their departure was in both cases well timed for William. The French king had produced two sons but the eldest, Philip, was only eight at the time of his father's death. Geoffrey, meanwhile, had fathered no children at all, and Anjou was plunged into a succession dispute between two of his nephews. For the first time in nearly a decade, Normandy was free from external threat.

William sought to capitalize on his neighbours' weakness. With Martel gone, he set out to expand his own power further into Maine. When the Count of Maine, Herbert II, died in March 1062, William claimed the region as his own. The pro-Angevin party in Le Mans preferred an alternative candidate in the shape of Herbert's uncle, but were powerless to resist Norman military pressure. William repeatedly harried the countryside around Le Mans until its citizens surrendered, and by the end of the year the whole county was in his hands.[11]

The duke's confidence at this point in his career is reflected by the way in which he developed the town of Caen in central Normandy, transforming it from a settlement of no significance into a rival to the duchy's capital at Rouen. On an outcrop of rock in the middle of the town he raised a giant castle, and in 1063 he founded a new monastery outside the town walls dedicated to Saint Stephen. During William's lifetime Normandy had witnessed a remarkable religious renaissance. Lay aristocrats competed with each other to found new religious houses, establishing no fewer than fourteen in the short time since the Battle of Val-ès-Dunes. The duchy's bishops were tearing down their old cathedrals and replacing them with magnificent new ones, built in the same Romanesque style as Edward the Confessor's Westminster Abbey, and in some cases travelling to Italy to raise the necessary funds. Scholars were flooding into Normandy to sit at the feet of internationally renowned intellectuals such as Lanfranc, a Lombard monk who had transformed the fledgling abbey of Bec into the most celebrated seat of learning in Europe. Lanfranc had also acquired the role of spiritual adviser to the duke himself, who, in the words of William of Poitiers, 'entrusted to him the direction of his soul, and placed him on a lofty eminence from which he could watch over the clergy throughout the whole of Normandy'. After a certain amount of arm-twisting, Lanfranc agreed to become the first abbot of William's new abbey of St Étienne.[12]

In the twelve years since his visit to England William had been preoccupied with defending his duchy from attack and consolidating his power in northern France. If he had contact with anyone across the Channel during this time, no record of it has survived. In 1064 or 1065, however, the situation changed dramatically, with the arrival in Normandy of England's most powerful earl.

5
Earl Harold

Earl Godwine had little time to relish his restoration to power. On Easter Monday 1053, barely seven months after his triumphant return to England, he was sitting down to dinner at Winchester with Edward the Confessor, his now dutiful son-in-law, when he suddenly sank towards the ground, 'bereft of speech and deprived of all his strength'. The *Anglo-Saxon Chronicle* goes on to explain how the earl was carried into a private chamber in the hope that he might recover, but died three days later. He was buried in Winchester's Old Minster, alongside the bones of his former master, King Cnut.[1]

Godwine's departure, however, did not arrest the rise of his descendants. The earl had fathered no fewer than six sons, five of whom were still living in 1053. He was succeeded in Wessex by the eldest survivor, Harold, who up to that point had been Earl of East Anglia. Sadly, no contemporary biography of Harold has survived, but he is described in *The Life of King Edward* as being wise, patient and merciful, strong in mind and body, 'a true friend of his race and country'. Such praise is hardly surprising, since the *Life* was commissioned by his sister, Queen Edith, and was intended to celebrate the rise of her family rather than the career of her husband. And there was plenty to celebrate. In 1055 Harold's younger brother Tostig was appointed as the new Earl of Northumbria, a move which involved passing over the son of the previous incumbent. In 1057 another brother, Gyrth, became the new Earl of East Anglia, and in 1058 an earldom in the south-west Midlands was found for a fourth brother, Leofwine. In the five years since their father's death the Godwinesons had come to dominate England like no other family before or since.[2]

There was evidently some resistance to this takeover. *The Life of King Edward* says that Tostig was appointed 'with no opposition from the king', a clumsy rebuttal that implies the Confessor may well have objected to the promotion of another Godwineson. But after the family's forceful return in 1052 Edward was essentially a broken reed, lacking the power and authority required to contradict his over-mighty in-laws. The *Life* paints a fairly pathetic picture of him in retreat from the world, passing his days in hunting or in prayer, happy in the knowledge that his realm was being run by Harold and Tostig. More robust opposition came from Ælfgar, Earl of Mercia, who during these five years was twice sent into exile, only to reassert himself on both occasions by linking arms with the Welsh. But by 1062 Ælfgar was dead, leaving his Welsh allies exposed to retribution. The following year Harold and Tostig invaded Wales, and the Welsh king, Gruffudd ap Llywelyn, was killed by his own men. His severed head was sent to Edward the Confessor, but all over Wales memorial stones were erected announcing that this was

Harold's victory. No one can have been in any doubt about who was really running the country.[3]

Throughout this period the question of the succession loomed larger than ever, for the marriage of Edward and Edith remained childless. For a time in the mid 1050s there was a sustained effort by some members of the king's court to locate another descendant of the house of Wessex, a grandson of Æthelred the Unready who had grown up in distant Hungary. Edward the Exile, as he was dubbed by later historians, returned home in the spring of 1057, only to die almost immediately, in obscure circumstances that the *Anglo-Saxon Chronicle* clearly considered suspicious. But he left a son of his own, probably about five years old, named Edgar, who was described as 'ætheling' in some sources, a title that meant he was throne-worthy. For those who believed that legitimacy was conferred by blood, he clearly had the best claim to be England's next king.[4]

If the tumults of the eleventh century had taught the English anything, however, it was that a hereditary claim to power could easily by trumped by other factors. Violence was one, as the Vikings had shown. Virtue was another. The Godwines, who had risen in the first instance by siding with the Danes, owed their success to both these qualities, though they naturally preferred to emphasize the latter. They had been aiming at the throne ever since old Earl Godwine had married his daughter to Edward the Confessor in 1045. Almost two decades on, having extended their power across most of England, they were unlikely to let the appearance of an inconvenient child frustrate their long-nurtured plan. *The Life of King*

Edward, in reality a tract in praise of the Godwines, reads like propaganda intended to prepare England for an imminent change of ruling dynasty.

This background is crucial to understanding the trip that Harold made to Normandy, probably in 1064. Norman sources, such as William of Poitiers, insist that the earl crossed the Channel in order to reaffirm Edward's earlier promise of the succession to Duke William. But this seems utterly incredible, for by this stage the Confessor was clearly in no position to command Harold to do anything, let alone oblige him to carry out a mission that would have been highly detrimental to his own interests. Most English sources make no mention of the trip at all, and those that do offer explanations that seem equally unlikely. According to the Anglo-Norman William of Malmesbury, writing half a century later, some Englishmen argued that Harold had ended up in Normandy by accident, and had set out to go fishing.[5]

The best explanation, in terms of fitting with the known political circumstances, is provided by a monk of Canterbury called Eadmer, who wrote in the early twelfth century. In Eadmer's version of events, Harold travelled to Normandy at his own initiative in order to negotiate the release of members of his own family whom William was holding hostage. The existence of the hostages is well attested by other sources – even William of Poitiers found it impossible to avoid mentioning them. They had been surrendered by the Godwine family at some point during the crisis of 1051–2 and transferred to William's custody.

Eadmer names them as Wulfnoth, the last of Harold's younger brothers, and Hakon, the son of Harold's older brother, Swein, who had died in 1052.[6]

A mission on Harold's part to liberate his brother and nephew seems very plausible. It would have been highly embarrassing for the earl that, despite his great power, two of his closest kinsmen were being detained by a foreign duke. More to the point, if he was contemplating a bid for the English throne, ensuring that his relatives were beyond harm's reach would have been a necessary preliminary step. Eadmer implies that Harold's plan may have been to buy William off, for he says that the earl took with him large quantities of gold, silver and costly goods.[7]

So, probably in the spring of 1064, Harold set out. His adventure is well known because it forms the opening part of the Bayeux Tapestry, which begins with a conversation between the earl and his brother-in-law, the king (though, as usual with the Tapestry, we are left to guess what they might be saying). Harold then rides with his retainers to his manor of Bosham in Sussex, where they put to sea. Landing by mistake in Ponthieu (other sources suggest they were blown there by a storm), they are captured by the local count, Guy. William, however, soon discovers what has happened and commands Guy to bring his English visitors to Normandy.[8]

Once in Normandy, the Tapestry depicts Harold doing two things. Firstly, he goes on campaign with William, participating in a short war against Brittany, Normandy's western neighbour. Secondly, he swears an oath to William, promising to uphold the duke's claim to England.

Both these activities are supported by other sources, including William of Poitiers, who describes the Breton campaign at some length. Fighting in Brittany together suggests that relations between the earl and the duke were friendly and collaborative; the Tapestry even has Harold heroically rescuing a couple of Norman soldiers who have managed to get stuck in some quicksand. The oath, however, can hardly have been taken unless Harold was acting under duress. Poitiers's insistence that the earl swore it 'clearly and of his own free will' suggests the truth lay in the opposite direction. According to Eadmer, the earl 'could not see any way of escape without agreeing to all that William wished'.

And what did William wish? Eadmer and Poitiers offer very similar descriptions. Harold agreed to become the duke's vassal, and pledged his personal support for William's claim to the throne when the time arose. He also promised to strengthen Dover Castle and garrison it with his own men for the duke's use, as well as other places throughout the rest of England. Eadmer adds that Harold also agreed to marry one of William's daughters.

Harold's plan thus spectacularly backfired. Far from persuading William to abandon his claim to the English succession, he had actually given the duke the opportunity to strengthen his hand. William, canny as ever, agreed to let his English guest take home his nephew, Hakon, but kept his brother, Wulfnoth, as a continued guarantee of the earl's good faith. When Harold eventually returned to England, says Eadmer, Edward the Confessor chided him for his naivety, saying 'Did I not tell you that I knew

William, and that your going might bring untold calamity on this kingdom?'[9]

And calamity was indeed quick in coming, though from a direction that neither man expected. In the autumn of 1065 the people of northern England rose up against Harold's brother Tostig, incensed by his harsh rule and his execution of his political enemies. In his place they appointed a young man named Morcar, the younger son of the late Earl Ælfgar, and joined forces with Ælfgar's other son, Eadwine, who had succeeded to the earldom of Mercia. A general uprising against the hegemony of the Godwinesons was under way, and the men of Northumbria and Mercia harried and burned their way as far south as Oxford. Dramatic scenes followed at Edward's court when Harold refused to raise the men of Wessex to fight in what would have been a disastrous civil war, prompting Tostig to accuse his older brother of being in league with the rebels. The discord was all too much for Edward the Confessor, now in his early sixties, who fell into a sickness from which he never recovered. A few days after Christmas he died at his palace in Westminster, and was buried in the magnificent abbey he had spent most of his reign rebuilding. The funeral took place on 6 January 1066, and was immediately followed by the coronation of King Harold.[10]

6
The Road to Hastings

The news that Harold had been crowned did not go down well in Normandy. The 'mad Englishman', said William of Poitiers, had 'violated his oath and seized the throne . . . with the connivance of a few wicked men'. In fact Harold, by far the most powerful man in England even before his accession, must have enjoyed the support of the majority of the kingdom's other magnates. Some English sources insist he had been nominated by the dying Confessor and elected with universal magnate consent. Others are more cagey, speaking only of Edward entrusting or commending the kingdom to Harold's protection. But if anyone did question the validity of Harold's claim, or wonder about the rights of young Edgar Ætheling, they were evidently overruled. The new king obtained the backing of his former rivals, the brother earls Eadwine and Morcar, by taking their sister, Ealdgyth, as his queen, abandoning his existing wife, Edith Swan-Neck, in order to do so.[1]

With Harold's rule apparently securely established, the only way for William to pursue his claim was by mounting a cross-Channel invasion. But as the earlier adventures of Edward the Confessor had shown, this was a high-risk enterprise, quite unlike the more cautious methods of warfare that the duke had practised up to this point. That William was prepared to take this gamble, and potentially lose all that he had already gained, suggests he believed his own rhetoric about the righteousness of his claim. To trust to the waves and the weather, and to confront Harold in open battle, would be to put the question of the English succession to the judgement of God. One of the first steps that William took in 1066 was to send an embassy to Rome in the hope of obtaining the blessing of the pope. Alexander II responded favourably, signalling his approval by sending the duke a banner, decorated with the cross of Saint Peter, which could be borne into battle.[2]

Other people apparently took longer to convince. During the early months of the year, William had an uphill struggle persuading the magnates of Normandy to participate in the planned invasion. There were initial meetings between the duke and his greatest vassals, and then larger assemblies in which he strove to win over the duchy's lesser lords and knights, some of whom argued that they were not obliged to serve beyond the sea. Bargains were struck, arms were twisted, and all were tempted by the promise of fabulous reward, should they succeed. The leading magnates each undertook to provide a certain number of men and ships. Across the whole province trees were felled in their thousands and shipwrights set to work to build the necessary armada. For a whole week at the end of April, Halley's comet blazed across the night sky. 'Many people said it portended a change in some kingdom', said William of Jumièges. William of Poitiers called it the 'terror of kings' and explained it as a sign of Harold's impending doom.[3]

Just days after the comet had disappeared, England was disturbed by the reappearance of Harold's younger brother, Tostig. The exiled earl raided along the south and east coasts, doing a great deal of damage, seizing some men and slaying many others, before eventually withdrawing to Scotland. His objective is mysterious, so it is unclear whether he was hoping to unseat Harold or to force his own readmission, much as their father had done fifteen years earlier. A later chronicler, Orderic Vitalis, believed that Tostig had been sent by William, presumably to soften up the English defences. Harold himself reportedly interpreted his brother's attack as a sign that a Norman invasion was imminent, and responded by mustering his own forces. According to the *Anglo-Saxon Chronicle*, he 'gathered together greater naval and land levies than any king in this country had ever gathered before'. After spending some time on the Kent coast at Sandwich, Harold sailed to the Isle of Wight and spread his forces along the south coast, waiting for the first sighting of enemy sails.[4]

But the expected invader failed to materialize. As spring turned to summer, William's preparations were indeed nearing completion. On 18 June the duke made another bid for divine assistance by attending the dedication of the new abbey of Holy Trinity in Caen, founded by his wife Matilda seven years earlier, and by the beginning of August, if not before, some 700 ships were assembled at the nearby port of Dives-sur-Mer, ready to convey the army of around 7,000 men who were camped in the surrounding countryside. They could not set sail, however, because of the atrocious weather. 'For a long time tempest

and continuous rain prevented your fleet from sailing' said
the anonymous author of *The Song of the Battle of Hastings*, a contemporary poem addressed to William himself,
and thus worth taking seriously. Some modern historians
have dismissed this testimony, arguing that the duke was
deliberately delaying his departure, waiting for Harold's
army to run into logistical difficulties that would force it to
disband. The problem with this argument, of course, is
that William faced exactly the same difficulties in keeping
his own forces supplied from one week to the next. Every
day he delayed required him to find vast quantities of food
and water to sustain all his men and horses (and to remove
vast quantities of waste that would otherwise have caused
death and disease). The more reasonable conclusion is that
the author of the *Song* was telling the truth, and that the
duke was genuinely 'in despair when all hope of sailing
was denied'.[5]

As summer turned to autumn, events suddenly sped up.
On 8 September Harold was indeed forced to disband his
army and sent his fleet back to London. 'The men's provi-
sions had run out,' explains the *Anglo-Saxon Chronicle*,
'and no one could keep them there any longer.' Then,
around four or five days later, William and the Normans
put to sea. The timing is unlikely to have been a coinci-
dence, and suggests that the duke had heard the news from
England and decided that it was too good an opportunity
to miss. But the weather was still against him, and
William's desperate gamble nearly cost him the whole
campaign. 'The rough sea compelled you to turn back',
says the *Song*, explaining how the Norman fleet was driven

along the rocky coast of northern France, finally finding a safe harbour at St Valéry-sur-Somme, 100 miles to the east, in the territory of the Count of Ponthieu. It was a near-disaster. William of Poitiers writes of 'terrible ship-wrecks', men drowned at sea and the survivors beginning to desert from the duke's army. The wind, moreover, continued to blow in the wrong direction, and prevented any thought of setting out for a second time. All they could do was pray to God and St Valéry, whose body was removed from the local church and paraded before the disheartened troops in the hope of reviving their spirits and their fortunes.[6]

While they prayed and waited, more dramatic news arrived. Around the same time as their departure from Dives, the irrepressible Earl Tostig had returned to England, this time bringing with him a large army led by the fearsome King of Norway, Harold Hardrada. This development seems to have come as a complete surprise both to the English and the Normans, with chroniclers in both countries describing it as unexpected. Tostig appears to have visited Scandinavia at some point during the spring or summer and convinced Hardrada, a legendary warrior around fifty years old, that England was ripe for a Viking reconquest. The two of them had landed in Northumbria in the first week of September, defeated local levies led by Earls Eadwine and Morcar, and occupied the city of York. Harold Godwineson, having disbanded his forces on 8 September, unaware of his brother's invasion, was now rapidly trying to reassemble an army, and had already set out north to counter this new threat.[7]

At last, after a fortnight of waiting at St Valéry, the

weather broke and the wind changed direction. The Norman army erupted in rejoicing and made immediate preparations to embark. *The Song of the Battle of Hastings* vividly captures the frantic scene, with men rushing to stow their weapons, horses being urged onto ships and sails being hoisted. It was late in the day when they finally put to sea, and as the sky filled with stars the fleet was lit by a thousand torches. This time the voyage was far less eventful, the only drama occurring when William's ship sped so far ahead that its crew lost sight of the others. William of Poitiers explains how the duke, unflappable as ever, calmly enjoyed a hearty breakfast, accompanied by spiced wine, confidently predicting that the other ships would soon materialize – as indeed they did.[8]

The next morning – probably 28 September, just possibly the day after – they landed in England. Disembarking at Pevensey in Sussex, almost certainly by design, they occupied its ancient Roman fort and raced to secure nearby Hastings, where an Iron Age hill fort offered similar protection. But for the moment such defences were unnecessary, for their arrival was unopposed. Every available English warrior had been summoned to Yorkshire to resist the invasion of Harold Hardrada. Remarkably, when William and his followers first set foot in England, they had no idea which King Harold they would end up having to fight. Only a day or so later did they learn that Harold Godwineson had won a great victory, surprising and killing Hardrada and Tostig on 25 September at Stamford Bridge, a battle so decisive and merciless that the Humber is said to have run red with Viking gore. The messenger who related this news to William, sent by a sympathetic servant of the late Edward the Confessor, warned that the triumphant Harold was hastening southwards to deal similarly with the Normans, and advised the duke to remain behind his fortifications rather than offer battle.[9]

But on this occasion avoiding battle was not an option. William's supplies were limited and his troops had their backs to the sea. The success of his strategy depended on confronting and defeating Harold as quickly as possible. As soon as the Normans had landed they had begun harrying the Sussex countryside, partly to secure more food but also as a provocation, hoping that the English king would hurry south to defend his people.

Harold rose to the bait. It is very likely that he was still in Yorkshire when news of the Norman landing reached him around the start of October. It is also very likely that he had dismissed the bulk of his army soon after their victory at Stamford Bridge. For the second time in a month, therefore, the king was forced to recall his levies from the shires, urging them to reassemble in London with all speed as he and his household troops rode back south. Once he arrived in London Harold could have afforded to pause but, according to the *Anglo-Saxon Chronicle*, he set out precipitately, 'before all his host had come up'. As William of Poitiers explains, the furious king hurried towards Hastings 'because he had heard that the lands near to the Norman camp were being laid waste'. But there was also another reason for his alacrity. As in Yorkshire, he was hopeful that by moving quickly he would take his enemies 'in a surprise or night-time attack'.[10]

William, however, had deployed scouts to warn him of such a strategy, and got wind of Harold's approach. On 13 October he ordered his army at Hastings to stand to arms throughout the night, and at dawn the next day they set out in search of their foe. William in this way turned the tables on his opponent, surprising the English king at a place about seven miles north-west of Hastings that the *Anglo-Saxon Chronicle* called 'the grey apple tree'. Today it is known as Battle.[11]

Our only detailed sources for what followed are *The Song of the Battle of Hastings* and William of Poitiers – the works of a poet and a propagandist, neither of whom was present on the battlefield. Nevertheless, by comparing and contrasting their accounts, a reasonable picture of what happened can be reconstructed in broad outline. When the two sides saw each other, we are told, there was a sudden rush to arms – so sudden that William, in his haste, put on his mailshirt the wrong way round, a mistake that many around him took as a bad omen, but which the duke is said to have laughed off.[12]

More ominous for the Normans was the fact that their enemies had command of the high ground, and were deployed along the length of a ridge in a line several men deep, forming the famous 'shield-wall' long favoured by English and Scandinavian armies, at the centre of which Harold raised his standard. At the foot of the hill the Normans were drawn up in three divisions, consisting of archers, infantry and cavalry – not the order that William had wanted, according to the *Song*. The presence of archers in the Norman ranks, however, was crucial, for the

English appear to have had no comparable complement of bowmen.[13]

The battle began with a shower of arrows falling on the English, killing some, maiming others, but failing to break the shield-wall. Next came a clash of arms as the Norman infantry ran up the hill to engage their opponents in hand-to-hand fighting, only to be beaten back with a hail of javelins and throwing-axes. The Norman cavalry rushed in to help, but the steepness of the slope and the roughness of the ground prevented them from mounting an effective charge, so they too were forced to engage at close quarters, leading to heavy losses. The English, says Poitiers, 'drove back those who dared to attack them with drawn swords'. The shield-wall held.[14]

Then, after hours of such bloody and exhausting attacks, a decisive turning point occurred. During one of these Norman assaults some horsemen on William's left wing ran away, and the duke's battle line started to collapse. Our two principal sources disagree as to whether this was a genuine retreat or a ruse that went wrong, but both agree that it nearly lost the battle for the invaders. A rumour flew through the Norman army that William himself had been killed, prompting the duke to ride around with his helmet removed to demonstrate that this was not the case.

However it came about, this near-disaster handed the Normans a critical advantage, because when several of their number started to flee some of the English pursued them down the hill, thinking that the battle was won, and in so doing abandoned the high ground and compromised the integrity of the shield-wall. Once the Normans had recovered their composure they were able to wheel round and slaughter their pursuers, and found that they were able to outflank and encircle the diminished English line. Again the sky was filled with arrows and more Englishmen fell.[15]

Among the fallen was King Harold. Whether or not he was hit in the eye by an arrow, as later chroniclers and history books would claim, can now never be known for sure. The only contemporary source to suggest as much is the Bayeux Tapestry, in a scene which is open to various interpretations and which was heavily restored in the nineteenth century. *The Song of the Battle of Hastings*, by contrast, describes how the king was hacked down by a dedicated Norman death squad, led by William himself. The fact that William of Poitiers, who wrote with a copy of the *Song* in front of him, omits this scene altogether and fails to offer an alternative explanation of how Harold met his end might be taken as an unwitting endorsement. However it came to pass, the death of the English king meant a decisive victory for the Normans and their duke. As the long and bloody day drew to a close, the cry 'Harold is dead!' sounded across the battlefield, and the surviving English fled.[16]

7
Resistance

William woke on the morning after the battle to survey the scene of his victory. 'Far and wide', wrote his chaplain, 'the earth was covered with the flower of English nobility and youth, drenched in blood.' Among them were Harold's younger brothers, Leofwine and Gyrth, whose bodies were found lying close to that of the dead king himself. With his main rivals annihilated, the duke ordered his own dead to be buried and then returned to Hastings, where he waited with his army in confident expectation that the remaining members of the English elite would submit and recognize him as their rightful ruler.[1]

But no submissions came. After a week or so of waiting, William learned that the English were rallying to London and preparing for further resistance. Led by Ealdred, Archbishop of York, the Londoners had elected Edgar Ætheling, last survivor of the royal house of Wessex, as their new king. ('As indeed was his right by birth', said the *Anglo-Saxon Chronicle*.) The young Earls of Mercia and Northumbria, Eadwine and Morcar, had given Edgar their backing and sworn to fight for him.

And so the Norman campaign continued. William marched eastwards along the coast, securing the ports of

Sussex and Kent, allowing his troops to burn and plunder as they pleased. Dover surrendered without a struggle, as did Canterbury, while a detachment of Normans was sent to seize Winchester, the ancient capital of Wessex and location of the royal treasury. Their success was rapid, but nothing about the outcome was preordained. At Dover many of William's men died from dysentery as a result of eating unsuitable food, and for a time the duke himself fell ill – a 'What-If?' moment in English history if ever there was one.[2]

Once he had recovered William advanced towards London, but the city was protected by the River Thames, which could be crossed only by London Bridge, and the bridge was held against him. After burning Southwark he moved westwards along the river's south bank, harrying his way through Surrey, Hampshire and Berkshire, until at last he reached Wallingford in Oxfordshire, where he and his men were able to cross the Thames unopposed and approach London from the north. By this point those holding the capital were feeling less sure of themselves, not least because Eadwine and Morcar had retired to their earldoms, taking their own troops with them and leaving the Londoners to their fate. A short time later a crowd of citizens, magnates and bishops, including Archbishop Ealdred and Edgar Ætheling, made their way to William's camp at Berkhamsted in Hertfordshire and offered their surrender. As the final days of the year drew in, the duke entered London in order to be crowned.[3]

As we have seen, William's coronation did not go as smoothly as he would have wished. Having claimed his own prize, however, the king was able to start rewarding his followers. In the preceding weeks he had been collecting tribute from towns and cities as they surrendered, and this accumulated loot was now redistributed. Much of it, of course, went to the military men who had helped him win the battle, but a great deal was sent to monasteries in Normandy who had supported him with prayers. A large amount of gold and silver was also sent to Pope Alexander II in recognition of his blessing of the invasion, including a gold-embroidered banner that had belonged to King Harold.[4]

At the same time William attempted to settle urgent questions about land. The estates of Englishmen who had fought against him at Hastings were deemed forfeit, and reallocated among his Norman followers. His half-brother, Odo of Bayeux, was made Earl of Kent, and his lifelong friend William fitz Osbern received much of Hampshire as well as the Isle of Wight. Those Englishmen who surrendered after the battle, however, found they were able to retain their property in exchange for payment. Among those who struck such a deal were Eadwine and Morcar, who submitted soon after the coronation, and in return had their lands and titles confirmed. William's desire at the start of his reign was to be seen not as a conqueror, but as the legitimate heir of Edward the Confessor. A letter written during the early weeks of 1067 assured the citizens of London that their laws and customs would remain as they had been during the Confessor's day. The new king's hope was apparently to rule a realm in which Normans and Englishmen could peacefully coexist.[5]

In March 1067, six months after his victory, William

returned to Normandy and a rapturous homecoming. People crowded to see him wherever he went, and lined the streets of Rouen to shout out his name. Their former duke, now a king, presented a dazzling spectacle, dressed, like his courtiers, in robes encrusted with gold, and accompanied by exotic, long-haired English nobles who had been brought as hostages. The festival atmosphere continued throughout the spring and into the summer, with feasting, gift-giving and the dedication of new churches.[6]

In England, meanwhile, William's regents struggled with the more difficult task of governing his newly conquered kingdom. Odo of Bayeux and William fitz Osbern, said William of Poitiers, 'burned with a common desire to keep the Christian people in peace [and] paid the greatest respect to justice'. But the half-English Orderic Vitalis, who copied freely from Poitiers to produce his own chronicle, begged to differ. The king's vicegerents, he maintained, 'were so swollen with pride that they would not deign to hear the reasonable plea of the English, or give them impartial judgement', and protected Norman soldiers who were guilty of plunder and rape. One thing that both writers agreed on, however, was that the regents had been busy building castles. Only a tiny handful of these new-fangled, French-style fortifications had been established in England before 1066, but now the English were experiencing a profound shock as scores of new ones were thrown up all over the country. 'Bishop Odo and Earl William', said the *Anglo-Saxon Chronicle*, 'built castles far and wide throughout the land, oppressing the unhappy people.'[7]

Norman oppression bred English resistance. During the

summer of 1067 there were disturbances along the Welsh border and a rising in Kent supported by the Count of Boulogne, both of which the regents were able to crush or contain. But towards the end of the year fears of a more widespread conspiracy prompted William to return and deal with the situation in person. At the start of 1068 he marched into the West Country to crush a rebellion fomented by Harold's mother, Gytha, and the surviving remnants of the Godwine family, laying siege to Exeter and planting a new castle in the city after its surrender. Believing the tumult had been quelled, the king celebrated Easter in London and sent for his wife, Matilda, who was crowned as England's new queen at Whitsun. During the summer, however, another co-ordinated revolt broke out in the Midlands and northern England, led by Eadwine and Morcar, championing the cause of Edgar Ætheling. Again the king responded swiftly and violently, leading his army on a devastating progress as far as the Humber and establishing new castles at Warwick, Nottingham, York, Lincoln, Huntingdon and Cambridge. The two earls swiftly buckled and sued for peace, while Edgar fled to take refuge with the King of Scots. By the end of the summer the country again seemed secure enough for William to risk returning to Normandy.[8]

The reality was that the king was caught in a vicious circle of his own making. By confiscating the lands of the English who had opposed him at Hastings, and using them to provide for his Norman followers, he had created a class of resentful, dispossessed men; even those who died during the great battle had relatives whose expectations of inheritance had been dashed. England's earlier conquerors had dealt with such dangerous, disaffected individuals by the simpler expedient of having them killed. 'Cnut the Dane', said William of Poitiers, in an impassioned passage addressed to his English readers, 'slaughtered the noblest of your sons, young and old, with the utmost cruelty.' King William had by contrast chosen to treat his defeated opponents with clemency, hopeful of ruling a genuinely Anglo-Norman realm. In so doing he had given the impression that his conquest would be reversible, and made it all but inevitable that rebellion would follow. Rebellion was punished with more disinheritance, and led to more Normans being rewarded with land; more disinheritance added to the number of English desperadoes with no reason to lay down their weapons.[9]

It was no real surprise, therefore, that 1069 witnessed a new wave of uprisings, larger and more determined than before. The first occurred at the start of the year, provoked by William's appointment of a new Earl of Northumbria, Robert de Commines, who arrived in the region with an army of mercenaries and occupied Durham by force, only to be slaughtered by the Northumbrians the next morning, along with all his men. This triggered a new general rising across the North, and the return of Edgar Ætheling and his fellow exiles from Scotland, who attacked York and laid siege to its new Norman castle. William hurried back from the continent to suppress this insurrection, raising the siege and dispersing the rebels, and demonstrated his impatience by sacking much of the city, including its ancient cathedral. When he withdrew it was clearly in expectation of more trouble to come. A second castle was begun in York and William fitz Osbern was left behind to keep the fragile peace.[10]

The peace was shattered in the late summer by a second uprising, timed to coincide with a Viking invasion. The English rebels had been appealing for Scandinavian assistance ever since 1066, and at this point the King of Denmark, Swein Estrithson, decided to throw his hat into the ring, confident that popular support in northern England would grant him a good chance of success. Danish forces sailed up the Humber in August and quickly seized York, killing its Norman garrisons. The northern rebels joined with them, hailing them as liberators, while other rebellions erupted simultaneously in the West Country and along the Welsh border. William spent a desperate autumn marching his troops back and forth across the country, trying to stamp out these many fires, which together constituted the gravest threat to his rule to date. The southern and western risings were in due course crushed, but the Danes remained elusive, and despite retaking York in December the king found he could not get near their fleet.[11]

Faced with this impasse, and frustrated with the continued resistance of the North despite three gruelling campaigns, William decided to solve the problem by a different method. His first move was to strike a deal with the Danes, allowing them to remain in England during the winter and plunder along the coast, on condition that they departed the following spring. He then embarked on the second part of his plan, which was to make northern England untenable by any army, Danish or English. 'In his anger', wrote Orderic Vitalis, 'he commanded that all crops and herds, chattels and food of every kind be brought together and burned . . . so that the whole region north of the Humber might be stripped of all sustenance.' This episode, known to posterity as the Harrying of the North, was one of the most notorious incidents of William's career. Harrying itself was standard practice in medieval warfare, but the scale of the destruction visited upon northern England that winter had such terrible consequences that even contemporary writers felt it was exceptional and excessive. A widespread famine followed, with starving refugees dragging themselves into southern England, and even reports of cannibalism. Orderic put the death toll at over 100,000, and an analysis of Domesday data suggests he was probably correct. Writing half a century later, the half-English monk lambasted William for causing such indiscriminate death, lamented the suffering of the innocent and declared that God would punish the king for his 'brutal slaughter'.[12]

Brutal as it undoubtedly was, the Harrying was effective in bringing the rebellion of the North to an end. In the spring of 1070 King Swein of Denmark landed in Yorkshire, hopeful of leading the army he had sent the previous summer to victory. The Danes who had remained in England, however, were so depleted of resources that his invasion came to nothing, and a few weeks later he sailed for home. William in the meantime had been tightening his grip on his traumatized kingdom, receiving the submissions of some rebels, chasing others into exile and building more new castles in Chester and Stafford. Any former respect he had shown to English sensibilities was now absent. During Lent he plundered the country's monasteries to pay off his mercenaries, and shortly afterwards he purged the English Church of most of its native bishops and abbots, replacing them with foreign clerks from his own chapel. At Easter he was ceremoniously recrowned at Winchester by visiting papal legates to re-emphasize the God-given nature of his rule, and towards the end of the summer he returned once more to Normandy.[13]

Although the North remained silent, there was one final English rising. In 1071 the Abbot of Ely, a monastery located in the fens of eastern England, became fearful that he too was about to be deposed and replaced. Resolving not to go quietly, he called in a renegade local lord named Hereward, who had gained notoriety the previous year by robbing the abbey at nearby Peterborough and allowing the Danes to make off with all its treasures. Soon other desperate men began to rally to Ely in the hope of making a last stand against the Normans, including the Bishop of Durham and several hundred English exiles from Scotland. Eadwine and Morcar also tried to raise rebellion, but found little support, and were quickly reduced to the status of outlaws. Eadwine indeed was betrayed and killed by his own men, so only Morcar made it as far as Ely.

This concentration of rebels was serious enough to draw William back to England in the summer of 1071, and he proceeded to mount a complicated siege, blockading the isolated town with boats and constructing a causeway across the marshes in order to mount an assault. Eventually the rebels were persuaded to surrender – tricked, according to Orderic, with false promises of renewed friendship. The reality was that William was past the stage of granting pardons in the hope of future obedience. Both Morcar and the Bishop of Durham were cast into prison for the rest of their lives (a long time, in the earl's case), while those of lesser status were mutilated, losing their hands and eyes. Only Hereward, it seems, realized that the king's change of heart meant surrender was not a sensible option, and led a band of men through the fens to safety, escaping into legend.[14]

8
Enemies Foreign and Domestic

The fall of Ely in 1071 marks an important turning point in William's life, and not just because it proved to be the last English rebellion against his rule. It was also at this moment that his contemporary biographer, William of Poitiers, decided to put down his pen, depriving us of our most detailed guide to his master's deeds and motives. Orderic Vitalis, who preserved the last part of Poitiers's chronicle by reworking it into his own, noted that his source had come to an end and vowed to continue as best he could, but Orderic was writing almost half a century later and offers nothing like the wealth of information provided by the Conqueror's own chaplain. Our knowledge of what William did for the rest of his career, therefore, is scanty compared to what we know of the earlier part.[1]

With rebellion in England apparently quelled, William was free to pay greater attention to the peripheries of his cross-Channel realm, and his first move was to invade Scotland. The Scottish king, Malcolm III, had been harbouring English fugitives since 1068, including the rival claimant to the throne, Edgar Ætheling, and at some point before 1070 he had demonstrated his commitment to their cause by marrying Edgar's sister, Margaret. In August

1072 William therefore set out to persuade Malcolm to change his mind, leading an army across the border and sending his fleet to mount a naval blockade. The Scottish king submitted at Abernethy on the banks of the River Tay, recognizing William as his overlord and handing over hostages, among them his eldest son, Duncan. Presumably Malcolm also promised to stop sheltering English rebels like his new brother-in-law, because the next time we encounter Edgar Ætheling he is residing at the court of the Count of Flanders.[2]

As this implies, William's relations with his Flemish in-laws had deteriorated sharply since his marriage to Matilda some twenty years earlier. In 1070 a succession dispute had broken out in Flanders between Matilda's nephew, Arnulf, and her brother, Robert. William had given his backing to Arnulf, but it was Robert who emerged victorious when the two sides met in battle in February 1071, killing not only his nephew but also the Conqueror's lifelong companion-in-arms, William fitz Osbern. From that point on, until the end of his reign, Flanders was for William what it had earlier been for Edward the Confessor: a hostile power, and a place of refuge for his enemies.[3]

Nor was the new Count of Flanders alone in his open hostility. In 1072 Robert married his half-sister, Bertha, to the young King of France, Philip I, newly emerged from the political tutelage that had proved so convenient for William in the 1060s, and now itching to revive the aggressive anti-Norman policy of his father. At the same time the new ruler of Anjou, Fulk Réchin, having won the struggle against his own brother, began to extend his power in a way not seen since the death of Geoffrey Martel. In the same year, responding to a request for help from the citizens of Le Mans, he invaded and occupied Maine, undoing the conquest that William had carried out a decade earlier. On the continent, the Conqueror was faced with a reversal of fortunes as enemies old and new combined against him on every side.[4]

William accordingly spent much more time in Normandy during the decade that followed than in England. In 1073 he crossed the Channel to recover Maine, taking with him a large army of Englishmen, who proved as efficient at harrying as their new overlords. 'They destroyed the vineyards, burnt down the houses and completely devastated the countryside,' says the *Anglo-Saxon Chronicle*, 'and brought it into subjection to the king.' William was in Normandy again the following year, this time concerned about the activities of Edgar Ætheling, who had been offered the French castle of Montreuil-sur-Mer by Philip I to serve as a base for attacks across the Norman border. On this occasion fortune favoured William, for Edgar returned to Scotland in order to marshal his resources but was shipwrecked on his voyage back to France, losing most of his men and almost all his treasure. As a result of this disaster, the young pretender reconsidered his position and decided it was time to make peace. Escorted by the sheriff of York, he made his way to Normandy and sought out the king, who, according to the *Chronicle*, 'received him with great ceremony'.[5]

Disappointed by Edgar's desertion, William's enemies sought other ways to undermine his power. In 1075 a new rebellion was launched in England, but led by foreign lords rather than the English themselves. Its instigator was a Breton named Ralph de Gaël, son of a favourite of Edward the Confessor, who had inherited the earldom of East Anglia by 1069. There was little love lost between the Bretons and the Normans, and since Ralph was later supported by the French king and the Count of Anjou, there is a good case for supposing that they were sponsoring his rebellion from the outset. The rising itself came to nothing, not least because the English, far from joining the revolt as anticipated, assisted William's regents in suppressing it. The king's spiritual mentor, Lanfranc of Bec, lately elevated to become the new Archbishop of Canterbury, wrote to his royal master in Normandy, enjoining him to stay put and assuring him that everything was under control: Ralph had fled to Brittany and his followers had been expelled. 'Glory be to God on high,' exclaimed England's most senior churchman, 'your kingdom has been purged of its Breton shit.'[6]

William did return to England later in 1075, drawn back by the renewed threat of Viking invasion, but this too proved to be a damp squib, and all the Danes succeeded in doing was sacking York. The king was thus able to spend Christmas handing out punishments to those who had participated in the recent rebellion, ordering some to be blinded and others banished. The two most significant rebels besides Ralph de Gaël were the Earl of Hereford, Roger of Breteuil and Waltheof, Earl of Northumbria. Their participation must have been gravely disappointing to William, for Roger was the eldest son of William fitz

Osbern, and Waltheof, despite his Anglo-Danish origins, had been shown special favour by being married to the king's niece. Roger was deprived of all his property and imprisoned for life, a harsh sentence but in keeping with William's practice of not killing noblemen who crossed him. Waltheof by contrast was kept in prison for six months and then summarily executed in the spring of 1076. Why William departed from his usual chivalrous restraint in the latter case is hard to explain. Orderic thought the differential treatment was due to the fact that Waltheof was an Englishman, and had been sentenced according to the 'law of England'.[7]

Orderic also felt that the subsequent misfortunes that befell the king were divine retribution for Waltheof's death. In the autumn of 1076 William crossed the Channel and invaded Brittany in pursuit of Ralph de Gaël, besieging the earl and some soldiers from Anjou in his castle at Dol. The siege, however, dragged on longer than expected, and after several weeks the king was forced to withdraw rapidly by the sudden arrival of Philip I, reportedly losing a great deal of men, horses and treasure. As a result William was obliged to agree a truce with both France and Anjou in 1077 on less than favourable terms.[8]

Worse was to follow later in the same year when the Conqueror fell out with his eldest son, Robert, whose own nickname was Curthose ('Shorty-Pants'). Born soon after his parents' marriage, Robert was in his mid twenties by 1077 and frustrated at his lack of independent power. In the autumn of that year, according to Orderic, he quarrelled with his younger brothers and rode off to Rouen, where he tried, without success, to seize the ducal castle. William was predictably furious and moved to attack his son, who responded by fleeing into the arms of his father's enemies, initially the Count of Flanders and eventually the King of France. It was a deeply damaging development, for Robert's own entourage included the sons of many of Normandy's most powerful magnates, and they accompanied him into exile. As earlier with Edgar Ætheling, the French king furnished his new protégé with a fortress close to the Norman frontier – in this case Gerberoy – from which to launch attacks into the duchy. William besieged it at the start of 1079, but once again experienced defeat when the garrison rode out to engage him. In the battle that followed the king's horse was killed from under him and he received a wound to the hand before sounding the retreat.[9]

The rift in the family threatened to grow deeper still when William discovered that his wife was secretly supporting Robert by sending him large sums of money. Orderic describes their ensuing row in some detail, most of which is inevitably invented. ('The wife who tricks her husband wrecks the home', exclaims an irate William at one point, improbably quoting Cato.) Yet Orderic undoubtedly captures an essential truth about their relationship when he has the king refer to Matilda as his helpmate, 'whom I have set over my kingdom and entrusted with all authority and riches'. William had indeed relied on his wife throughout his career to act as regent in Normandy during his repeated absences, as the charters issued in her name testify. According to Orderic, the king demonstrated his anger at the queen's betrayal by ordering one of her servants to be blinded, but the man in question received a timely tip-off and rushed off to seek sanctuary. He became a monk at Orderic's own monastery of St Evroul, suggesting that the story, although clearly much improved, had some basis in fact.[10]

If the row between William and Matilda was short-lived, the feud with Robert took longer to fix. Eventually, after repeated petitioning from Normandy's magnates and prelates, as well as the pleading of the queen, the king agreed to soften his stance and was reconciled with his errant son shortly before Easter 1080. The key condition, reported by Orderic, was William's confirmation that Robert would succeed him as Duke of Normandy. Scenes of general rejoicing throughout the duchy followed, for the rapprochement brought an end to several years of destructive civil war.[11]

With the royal family reunited, William was at last able to return his attention to affairs on the other side of the Channel. His half-brother, Odo of Bayeux, had been ruling England with an iron fist, and according to Orderic 'was dreaded by Englishmen everywhere'. When, for example, the Bishop of Durham was murdered by a mob in Northumbria in the summer of 1080, Odo subjected the region to a second round of harrying, and looted Durham Cathedral of all its treasures. A short time later the newly reconciled Robert Curthose was sent even further north to punish King Malcolm of Scotland, who had violated the terms of his earlier peace agreement by conducting raids across the border. Finally, towards the end of the year, William himself returned to England, making his first appearance in the kingdom for over four years. Following the tradition of Edward the Confessor, he celebrated Christmas at Gloucester, where he ceremoniously wore his crown.[12]

As well as being a good base for hunting in the Forest of Dean, Gloucester was also conveniently close to Wales, a region over which the Conqueror wished to cast a watchful eye. Welsh politics were extremely volatile, even by medieval standards, with almost constant fighting between rival ruling dynasties, and an occasional tendency to spill across the border into England. The southern frontier with Wales had originally been granted to William fitz Osbern, but after his untimely death in 1071 and the rebellion of his son in 1075, authority there had reverted to the Crown. When, therefore, the native rulers of south Wales fell into a fresh bout of bloody fighting at the start of 1081, and a new prince of untested loyalty emerged pre-eminent from the carnage, William felt compelled to restate his superior lordship. Raising an army of English soldiers, he advanced along the south Welsh coast as far as the Irish Sea, stopping at St David's to offer a pilgrim's prayer and planting a new castle at Cardiff as his army withdrew.[13]

It was also during this excursion into Wales that the king, in the words of the *Anglo-Saxon Chronicle*, 'freed many hundreds of people'. The Welsh, like the other indigenous peoples of Britain, still habitually kept and traded slaves. In England at least 10 per cent of the population, and possibly double that proportion, fell into this category, meaning that they had no protection from the law and could be beaten, branded, mutilated or killed as their

1. William, as Duke of Normandy, seated and holding a sword, depicted on the Bayeux Tapestry. The Tapestry was made soon after the Norman Conquest, most likely before 1082.

2. Harold Godwineson, returning to England from
Normandy, appears before Edward the Confessor.
The king appears to be admonishing the earl.

3. William's half-brother, Bishop Odo of Bayeux,
rushes into battle at Hastings to stop a Norman rout.
It was almost certainly Odo who commissioned the
Bayeux Tapestry.

4. An artist's impression of the wooden motte-and-bailey castle that William built at York after taking the city in 1068. Almost all early castles were made of earth and timber.

5. Workmen constructing a castle at Hastings immediately after the Norman landing in 1066.

6. St John's Chapel in the Tower of London. The site of the Tower was established shortly before William's coronation in 1066, and its great stone donjon was begun soon afterwards.

7. The great tower at Chepstow Castle, built soon after 1066, either by William himself or by his long-term friend and supporter, William fitz Osbern.

8. A plough team depicted in an eleventh-century Anglo-Saxon calendar. Many ploughmen were slaves in pre-Conquest England, but William abolished the slave trade.

9. A silver penny struck in William's reign, showing the king in profile.

10. A page from the Yorkshire section of Domesday Book. Many of the entries contain the word *vasta* (waste), on account of William's devastation of northern England in 1069–70.

9
Domesday

In 1085 it suddenly seemed possible that William's reign might be over in a matter of weeks, and that he would be replaced not by one of his sons but by another foreign conqueror. In the summer of that year news arrived that an invasion of England was being planned by the King of Denmark, Cnut IV, who had come to power five years earlier determined to replicate the success of his more celebrated predecessor and namesake. At the start of his reign this new King Cnut had forged an alliance with Robert of Flanders by marrying his daughter, Adele, and together the two men were assembling a massive armada. To judge from the comments of Ailnoth, a monk of Canterbury who later wrote a biography of the Danish king, at least some people in England were once again excited by the prospect of a new Scandinavian takeover that would bring an end to Norman tyranny.[1]

William, who was in Normandy when he heard the news, was reportedly 'very scared' by it, and responded by raising a massive army, perhaps even larger than the one with which he had conquered England in 1066. The difference was that on this occasion his troops were being asked not to devastate the country but to defend it, and this masters saw fit. Slave-raiding was regarded as a normal and acceptable part of warfare, with young men and women being routinely rounded up along with cattle as another form of booty. The Normans, by contrast, despite their Viking ancestry, had abandoned the practice of taking slaves in the half-century before the Conquest, and had come to regard the trade in human beings as unacceptably barbaric. William, for all the ferocity with which he waged war, had banned the slave trade at some point after his accession and, as the fleeting comment of the *Chronicle* suggests, was active in the process of liberating those who were held in bondage. It is one of the more remarkable and under-reported facts about the Norman takeover that, even as England's new rulers were making life more onerous for those who had previously been classed as free, they were improving the existence of men and women who had formerly been bought and sold like animals. 'In this respect,' observed the monk Lawrence of Durham in the 1130s, the English 'found foreigners treated them better than they had treated themselves.'[14]

With the fringes of his empire at peace and domestic harmony restored, William was at the height of his power in 1081, and appeared to contemporary observers as a great and glorious king. Some sense of the grandeur of his court is reflected in the building projects he had commissioned, such as the great stone keep that became known as the Tower of London, or the similar, squatter tower he built at Colchester in Essex. In Sussex, work was under way on a new abbey, known as Battle, to mark the spot where God had granted him victory and to atone for the bloodshed. In Winchester, where William wore his crown at Whitsun 1081, a new cathedral was rising that would dwarf not only its Anglo-Saxon predecessor but also every other church in Europe north of the Alps. Describing the state of England and Normandy at this moment, Orderic noted that it was 'a tranquil time'.[15]

But the years that followed brought renewed family discord. In 1082, to the astonishment of contemporary chroniclers, William arrested and imprisoned his half-brother Odo of Bayeux, the man who had ruled England, in Orderic's words, 'like a second king'. The bellicose bishop had apparently been plotting to make himself pope and recruiting knights to lead to Rome, a scheme that would have left the kingdom dangerously undefended. Placed on trial in the king's hall, he was said to have been seized by William himself, and spent the rest of the reign incarcerated in Rouen Castle.[16]

The following year the king suffered a blow even closer to home when Matilda fell sick and died on 2 November. Despite their quarrel over her clandestine support for Robert Curthose, the royal couple had remained on close and affectionate terms, and her death was said to have plunged William into the deepest mourning. It also, of course, deprived him of another individual whom he had been willing to trust as regent, and who was almost certainly the principal peacekeeper between the king and his eldest son. Shortly after Matilda's death Robert fell out with his father for a second time, and once again took himself off into exile. If this renewed rift was less damaging than it had been before, in that fewer men followed Robert's lead created major logistical difficulties. At an emergency council during the autumn it was decided that the best way to keep them supplied was to disperse them all over the kingdom, with some going to stay in towns and cities and others billeted in the households of magnates and bishops. William also ordered castles and town walls to be strengthened and the coast to be closely guarded; coastal regions were once again laid waste, so that the invaders would find no food if they landed.

Shortly before Christmas news arrived that the Danes had been delayed, and had put off their invasion until the following year. This gave William and his supporters a breathing space, and they used it to debate what should be done. That Christmas, which the king once again spent at Gloucester, he had what the *Anglo-Saxon Chronicle* calls 'much thought and deep discussion' with his council about the country, 'how it was occupied and with what sort of people'. The *Chronicle* then goes on to explain how as a result of this meeting men were sent into every shire to find out what everyone owned: how much land and cattle the king himself had, and how much was held by his bishops, abbots, magnates and all the other landowners. So thorough was this investigation, the *Chronicle* famously reported, that not one ox, cow or pig was left out of the resultant record.[2]

The investigation being described is, of course, the Domesday Survey, which led to the production of the Domesday Book, perhaps the most famous document in English history after Magna Carta. Originally bound as two books, containing some two million words, it has been justly called 'the most complete survey of a pre-industrial society anywhere in the world'. As the *Chronicle*'s comments suggest, contemporaries were struck by the scale of the enterprise. The name 'Domesday', explains a twelfth-century source, was a coinage of the English themselves, who compared the Conqueror's survey to Judgement Day.[3]

The puzzle for historians is why it was made at all. Clearly one purpose of the inquiry was to create a comprehensive record of land ownership, and to settle disputes about who owned what. The Domesday Book mentions around 13,000 places and some 30,000 individual lordly estates, or manors (a word introduced by the Normans them-selves). After twenty years of land redistribution, much of it chaotic, there was tenurial confusion everywhere. During the spring of 1086 special courts were convened across the country, at a county level as well as more locally, in which the claims of landowners were compared with the testimony of local jurors, who in many cases declared that they had no idea how a particular individual came to be holding his or her land.[4]

Establishing who owned what was an obvious prerequi-site for preventing feuding and fighting between neighbours with rival claims. It was also an essential first step for rais-ing more money, which was the other main reason behind the inquiry. The kings of Anglo-Saxon England had levied a land tax known as the *geld*, but its effectiveness had been eroded by exemptions. Some of these had been granted before 1066, but a great many more had been introduced in the twenty years since. At some stage during his reign, for example, it seems that William had excused his greatest subjects from having to pay, and had allowed them to keep the tax raised on their demesnes for themselves. In other cases land was excused from paying geld because it had been devastated during the Conquest and was now deemed 'waste' (*vasta*). More than 80 per cent of the total waste for the whole country occurs in Yorkshire, reflecting the terrible effectiveness of the Harrying of the North. Another cause of waste had been William's decision to set aside large areas of land as royal hunting preserves, or 'forest' – another word that was introduced after 1066. In Hampshire the king famously created the New Forest, extending an existing area of wilderness by around 20,000 acres, and clearing some 2,000 people off their land in order to do so.

The geld was thus nothing like the great cash-cow it had once been. Although William had levied it several times, and at eye-watering rates, these exemptions and erosions meant that its yield was low and disappointing. The inadequacy of the system may have been exposed in the autumn of 1085 by the decision to billet the king's mercenary army on individual magnates, 'each in proportion to his own land', as the *Anglo-Saxon Chronicle* puts it, a dispersal that would have been very unfair if based on geld lists. It is clear that part of the Domesday process was to collect data with a view to overhauling the tax system.

The problem is that the Domesday Book itself is completely unsuitable for assessing the incidence of geld. The commissioners who had compiled the data behaved like geld collectors, travelling from settlement to settlement and using local courts to obtain their information. But when it came to creating the Domesday Book this information was laboriously reorganized by individual landowners, making the calculation of geld liabilities almost impossibly complicated.[5]

What, then, was the purpose of the book? The answer is intimately bound up with a great ceremony that William organized in the summer of 1086, which seems to have been the climactic moment of the whole project. On 1 August, in compliance with the king's command, landowners from all over England assembled at Old Sarum in Wiltshire, an Iron Age hill fort that the Conqueror had transformed by the addition of a cathedral and a royal castle. To judge from the description of the chroniclers, who mention not only bishops, abbots and barons but also sheriffs, knights 'and all the landowners who were of any account', this was a very large gathering, probably several thousand strong. The reason for calling it was a great oath-taking ceremony. 'They all submitted to him,' says the *Anglo-Saxon Chronicle*, 'and became his men, and swore oaths of allegiance to him against all other men.' In other words, all the landowners in England did homage and swore fealty to William, recognizing him as their lord. In return the king was able to present them with the draft results of the Domesday Survey, which were almost certainly brought to him at this point.[6]

Each side gained something from this ceremony. For the landowners, it gave them much needed security of tenure. After years of confusion and violence, claim and counterclaim, a line was being drawn. If it was written down in the king's record, and you had performed homage for it, the land was unquestionably yours to hold. For the king's tenants, Domesday served as a giant title-deed or charter.

As for William, he gained recognition that all the land in his kingdom was ultimately held from the king – a concept not universally acknowledged in England before the Conquest. This meant that the king's lordship in future would be far more powerful, for those who held land from him had to recognize that they had certain obligations. In the first place, they were expected to render military service when he required it. It also meant that the king possessed a host of additional rights and powers over his tenants. When one of them died, for example, his heir had to pay the king in order to have the inheritance. If the heir was underage, the king became his guardian, and enjoyed the profits of the estate until the heir was old enough to inherit. The king also controlled the marriages of underage heirs and those of the widows of his deceased tenants. All these powers brought him a dependable stream of revenue, and also allowed him to determine the descent of aristocratic estates by marrying heirs and widows to men he wished to promote.

The purpose of the Domesday Book, it seems, was to help William and his successors work this system to their best advantage. The book is arranged as a directory of landowners. Knowing precisely who held what land, the king's ministers could direct his sheriffs to seize an estate when its tenant died, or if he rebelled. Knowing what it was worth, they could assess the scale of the sum (known as a 'relief') that an heir had to pay in order to inherit. The information contained in the book added considerably to

William's already extensive power, turning England into what has been called 'the most powerful royal lordship in medieval Europe'.[7]

The seven months that had elapsed since the launch of the Domesday Survey at the start of 1086 had clearly been terrible and calamitous. The *Anglo-Saxon Chronicle* writes of storms that destroyed the crops and widespread famine and pestilence, while other writers mention violence arising from the demand for royal taxes. But by the time of the great assembly at Old Sarum, the threat that seems to have triggered the whole project had passed. On 10 July 1086 William's would-be replacement, Cnut IV, was murdered by his own nobles while he knelt at prayer, removing the threat of foreign invasion.

As soon as the ceremony was over, therefore, William made preparations for his return to Normandy. From Wiltshire he went to the Isle of Wight, where he ordered yet another tax to be levied across England. He then took ship across the Channel, for what turned out to be the last time.[8]

10
Conclusion

Not long after his return to Normandy William fell ill, to the reported delight of his principal adversary. 'The king of England lies in Rouen,' laughed Philip I of France, 'like a woman who's just had a baby.' Such at least is the story told by William of Malmesbury, who explains that the Conqueror was laid up on account of his swollen stomach. Philip seized the opportunity to gain the military advantage, and sent his troops across the border to ravage the region around the Norman city of Évreux. By July 1087 William was sufficiently recovered to take his revenge and invaded the French king's lands, paying particular attention to the town of Mantes, which was mercilessly reduced to ashes. But in the course of this campaign William again fell sick, apparently from heat exhaustion, though some people, noted Malmesbury, said he was injured when his horse leaped over a ditch, driving the pommel of its saddle into his protruding abdomen.

By the time William returned to Rouen it was clear that he was dying, and a little while later, at his own request, he was moved away from the noise of the city to the church of St Gervase, a short distance beyond the walls. For the remainder of the summer he lingered there, in great pain, preparing for the end. Orderic Vitalis provides a lengthy account of these days, including the king's last words, most of which has to be rejected as invention forty years after the fact. William, we are told, spent much of his time confessing his sins, seeking to atone for a lifetime of bloodshed. He ordered that his treasure be divided among various churches after his death, and commanded that all prisoners still in his custody should be released. He also addressed the vexed issue of his succession, accepting that his rebellious eldest son, Robert Curthose, should follow him as Duke of Normandy, but apparently leaving the question open when it came to England. According to Orderic he refused to name an heir for the kingdom he had won with so much blood and entrusted the matter to God, a statement that draws support from the king's bequest of his regalia to the monks of St Étienne in Caen. William did, however, express a personal hope that the English crown would pass to his second surviving son, William Rufus.[1]

The Conqueror died early in the morning of 9 September 1087, reportedly commending his soul to Saint Mary as the great bell of Rouen Cathedral tolled the hour of prime (6 a.m.). His departure triggered immediate panic across Normandy, for Robert Curthose was still in exile, and the king's other sons had already rushed off to claim their own inheritances. With no one present to take up the reins of power, the great men who had been at William's bedside rode off to protect their own property, leaving the lesser members of his household to loot the royal lodgings. When the monks and clergy of Rouen eventually arrived at

St Gervase to prepare for the funeral, they found the king's body lying abandoned and half naked on the floor.

From Rouen William's corpse was shipped to Caen for burial, where it suffered further indignities. In a scene reminiscent of the king's coronation, the crowd of mourners who came to meet the boat dispersed when a fire broke out and destroyed much of the town, leaving only the monks to escort the bier to St Étienne. During the service itself the congregation was asked to forgive their dead duke if he had done them any wrong, at which a local man interrupted to complain that the abbey had been built on the site of his father's house. Finally, the king's body turned out to be too big for the stone sarcophagus that had been prepared for it, and the monks' attempt to force the issue caused his swollen bowels to burst, filling the church with such a stench that once again all except the officiating clergy fled.[2]

It was, as Orderic Vitalis observed, an ignominious end to the Conqueror's story (and as such a gift for a chronicler who wanted to show that God deals with princes and paupers in the same manner). Yet Orderic made no attempt to link these inglorious scenes to William's life, which in general he thought had been a good one. Although he reiterated his condemnation of the Harrying of the North, he began his obituary by describing the king as a peace-loving, God-fearing ruler, who had defended the Church and relied on the counsel of wise men. Others, however, found it more difficult to overlook the suffering that the Conquest had entailed. The German chronicler Wenric of Trier clearly had William foremost in mind when he condemned those contemporary rulers who had 'usurped kingdoms by the violence of a tyrant, paved the road to the throne with blood, placed a blood-stained crown on their heads, and established their rule with murder, rape, butchery and torment'.[3]

There is something to be said for both these views, though the truth lies somewhere between the two. The most interesting and arguably best-informed verdict on the Conqueror is provided by his obituary in the *Anglo-Saxon Chronicle*, written at some point before 1100.[4] 'If anyone desires to know what kind of man he was,' says the anonymous Englishman who composed it, 'then we shall write of him as we have known him, who have ourselves seen him, and at one time dwelt at his court.' The author goes on to describe William as 'a man of great wisdom and power', stronger than all his predecessors and 'stern beyond measure' to those who opposed him. Like Orderic he praised the king for protecting the Church and encouraging religion to flourish, and also for 'keeping great state' with regular crown-wearings. He also praised William for dealing robustly with his great men if they resisted him, and for keeping good order in general. The Domesday Survey is described with similar admiration, and so too the way in which William had imposed his authority on the rulers of Scotland and Wales.

But, as the Chronicler went on to explain, all this had come at a cost. The building of castles had been 'a sore burden to the poor', and the king's desire for money had led him to tax his subjects excessively, 'most unjustly and for little need'. He had also introduced the Forest and the

Forest Law, with draconian penalties for infringement. 'Assuredly,' said the Chronicler, 'in his time people suffered grievous oppression and manifold injuries.'[5]

Clearly this list of negatives is far from being comprehensive, but it is nevertheless interesting that, while the Chronicler describes William as being harsh, he does not accuse him of being cruel. Modern commentators, by contrast, have often condemned what they see as the king's excessive cruelty. By present standards, of course, some of the punishments that William dished out were savage: his maiming of the rebels who mocked him at Alençon and his mutilation and blinding of some English rebels in 1071 and 1075 would today be regarded as intolerable. What is far from clear, however, is whether William's conduct was regarded as exceptional in his own day, for the eleventh century was a cruel time. In Anglo-Saxon England, disobedient slaves were stoned to death if male, and burned to death if female. In praising William's maintenance of law and order, his English obituarist noted with approval the king's new policy of punishing rapists with castration.[6]

Some modern historians have seen evidence of the Conqueror pushing the boundaries of what was acceptable in the comments of Guibert of Nogent, a monk whose father had been captured fighting against William at some point in the 1050s. 'It had never been this count's habit to offer his captives for ransom,' Guibert noted, 'but instead he would condemn them to a life of perpetual imprisonment.' This was certainly true, for William did indeed incarcerate several men for a very long time. Those released as a result of his deathbed amnesty included his brother Odo, seized in 1082, Earl Roger of Hereford, sentenced in 1075, Earl Morcar, in prison since 1071, and even King Harold's younger brother, Wulfnoth, who had been handed over as a hostage as far back as 1051.[7]

From another perspective, however, what made William exceptional was not that he kept his prisoners for a long time, but that he bothered to imprison them in the first place. In England before 1066 the political elite had preferred to neutralize their opponents by killing them. The courts of Æthelred the Unready, Cnut, Harold Harefoot, Harthacnut and Edward the Confessor had all witnessed multiple political murders. In Normandy, too, there had been a spate of political killings fuelled by aristocratic feuding during William's minority. Historians who fancy themselves as psychologists often point to the duke's personal experience of this violence as a child to explain what they see as his exceptional brutality in later life, when in fact the evidence points to the opposite conclusion, for when William assumed personal power in Normandy the murders came to an end. Similarly, in England after 1066 political killing quickly became taboo. During William's reign only one high-ranking Englishman, Waltheof of Northumbria, was deliberately put to death on the king's orders, and thereafter no earl was executed in England until 1306. Far from making politics more cruel and bloody, the Conqueror had introduced a chivalrous attitude that would endure for more than two centuries.[8]

If there was a reason for William's restraint beyond a reaction to the events of his childhood, it was almost certainly a moral outlook that stemmed from the teachings of a reformed Church. From an early age he had been guided by Lanfranc of Bec, one of the greatest theologians in Europe, and according to William of Malmesbury he did everything that Lanfranc recommended, including ending the English slave trade. Malmesbury also noted that the king was a practising Christian 'as far as a layman could be, to the extent of attending mass every day, and every day hearing vespers and matins'. That William's religiosity was no mere outward show is indicated by his installation of Lanfranc as Archbishop of Canterbury and the equally reformist Maurilius as Archbishop of Rouen, as well as his frequent convening of Church councils. Pope Gregory VII, who as a cardinal had supported the invasion of England, admitted in a letter of 1081 that William was far from perfect, but noted that he had protected the Church, governed his subjects in peace and justice, supported the papacy and compelled married priests to put away their wives. 'In all these respects,' Gregory concluded, 'he has shown himself more worthy of honour and approbation than other kings.'[9]

As his enforcement of clerical celibacy suggests, William's piety, as guided by Lanfranc, had an almost puritanical streak, which may account for another noteworthy aspect of his personal life, namely his attitude to sex and marriage. The king had such respect for chastity, says William of Malmesbury, that before his marriage people whispered that he was impotent. Once he was married William soon disproved these rumours by fathering at least nine children. Significantly, however – and in sharp contrast to all his predecessors as dukes of Normandy, and all his twelfth-century successors as kings of England – he is not known to have fathered any illegitimate offspring. By the standards of his own age and class, William was unusually uxorious.[10]

Venturing beyond the opinions of contemporaries, we might speculate that William's attitudes here were conditioned by a sense of shame about his own illegitimacy. If this did not present a political obstacle to his accession as Duke of Normandy in 1035, it was clearly a cause of mockery in other parts of France, and became more embarrassing in the course of his own lifetime. Norman and Anglo-Norman chroniclers writing after the king's death, especially if they wanted to distinguish William from his namesake son, often referred to him as 'the Great'. ('The Conqueror' did not catch on until the thirteenth century.) But other chroniclers, writing in Germany, Scandinavia or elsewhere in France, routinely referred to him as 'the Bastard', as indeed did one version of the *Anglo-Saxon Chronicle* for the year 1066. William must have known of this nickname and is unlikely to have found it amusing. His sensitivity on the subject of his origins is well illustrated by his mutilation of the men who mocked his maternal ancestry at Alençon.[11]

Venturing further still, it is possible to see in William's whole career a lifelong desire for legitimacy, or at least to have his actions perceived as legitimate. He would not depose a bishop in England or Normandy without the participation of papal legates, nor would he embark upon the invasion of England without first securing the blessing of the pope. After the Conquest he took the extraordinary step of having the bishops of Normandy draw up a list of penances that the victors had to perform in order to atone for the bloodshed. Even the Domesday Book, practical as it was, testifies to the Conqueror's desire to legitimize his actions, presenting what had been a messy land-grab as a tidy legal transfer.[12]

To say this much is not to side with those who see William's appeal to the pope in 1066 as mere window-dressing, and who regard the Conquest as simply an exercise in freebooting, born of a residual Viking wanderlust or an insatiable appetite for expansion. Many men who participated in the invasion were enticed by the prospect of great riches, but it does not automatically follow that this was William's own attitude. Before 1066 his warfare had been for the most part cautious and defensive. He had enormous difficulty persuading many Normans to follow him to England, precisely because the venture was so insanely risky. To mount a seaborne invasion against a superior naval power, and to risk everything on the outcome of a single battle, was to put his cause before God and to stake his life, and the lives of thousands of others, on its justice. The reasonable conclusion is that William believed his cause to be just. He was not motivated by the spirit of speculative adventure that had brought his Viking forefathers to Normandy, or that tempted contemporary Scandinavian rulers to try their luck in England. His impetus seems rather to have stemmed from a warrior's mindset married to the conviction of religious zealot – a combination which within a decade of his death would spur other men eastwards in the hope of recovering Jerusalem.

It was this combination of martial skill and unshakeable faith that contributed to William's success. The belief that he was right, and that God was on his side, urged him on in situations where more pragmatic men might have cut their losses or altered their plans. Orderic Vitalis, almost certainly parroting the words of the Conqueror's chaplain, William of Poitiers, described how in 1070 the king led his troops across northern England in the depths of a bitter winter, ignoring their protests about the terrible weather and the lack of food, counting as cowards or weaklings those who deserted, and continuing with determination along a path that no horseman had ever attempted before. The author of the *Anglo-Saxon Chronicle*, with considerably more bitterness, rounded off his obituary of the king who had subjected England to such unprecedented trauma by poetically evoking the same quality:

> The rich complained and the poor lamented
> But he was too relentless to care, though all might hate him,
> And they were compelled, if they wanted
> To keep their lives and their lands
> And their goods and the favour of the king,
> To submit themselves entirely to his will.
> Alas, that any man should bear himself so proudly
> And deem himself exalted above all other men!
> May Almighty God show mercy to his soul
> And pardon him his sins.[13]

Notes

1. INTRODUCTION

1. *The Ecclesiastical History of Orderic Vitalis*, ed. M. Chibnall (6 vols, Oxford: Clarendon Press, 1968–80), vol. 2, pp. 182–5; *The Gesta Guillelmi of William of Poitiers*, ed. R. H. C. Davis and M. Chibnall (Oxford: Clarendon Press, 1998), pp. 146–7, 150–51; *The Anglo-Saxon Chronicle* (various editions), D, 1066.
2. *Anglo-Saxon Chronicle*, E, 1087; *Orderic Vitalis*, vol. 4, pp. 80–95.
3. D. C. Douglas, *William the Conqueror: The Norman Impact Upon England* (London: Methuen, 1964), p. 363; J. Dastague, 'Le Fémur de Guillaume le Conquérant: Étude Anthropologique', *Annales de Normandie*, 37 (1987), pp. 5–10; C. Dyer, *Standards of Living in the Later Middle Ages* (rev. edn, Cambridge: Cambridge University Press, 1998), p. 316; D. Carpenter, *Magna Carta* (London: Penguin, 2015), pp. 73–4; William of Malmesbury, *Gesta Regum Anglorum*, vol. 1, ed. and trans. R. A. B. Mynors, R. M. Thomson and M. Winterbottom (Oxford: Clarendon Press, 1998), pp. 508–11.

2. THE BASTARD

1. D. Crouch, *The Normans* (London: Hambledon, 2002), pp. 46–8; *The Gesta Normannorum Ducum of William of Jumièges, Orderic Vitalis and Robert of Torigni*, ed. E. M. C. van Houts (2 vols, Oxford: Clarendon Press, 1992–5), vol. 2, pp. 79–85; William of Malmesbury, *Gesta Regum*, pp. 426–7; E. M. C. van Houts, 'The Origins of Herleva, Mother of William the Conqueror', *English Historical Review*, 101 (1986), pp. 399–404.
2. *Rodulfus Glaber, Historiarum Libri Quinque*, ed. J. France, N. Bulst and P. Reynolds (2nd edn, Oxford: Clarendon Press, 1993), pp. 204–5.
3. M. Morris, *The Norman Conquest* (London: Hutchinson, 2012), pp. 15–16, 51–2.
4. Ibid., pp. 53–5; *William of Poitiers*, pp. 6–9.
5. Morris, *Norman Conquest*, pp. 44–6, 52–3, 55–7.
6. Ibid., pp. 66–8; *Gesta Normannorum Ducum*, vol. 2, pp. 128–9; *William of Poitiers*, pp. 30–31; J. Dewhurst, 'A Historical Obstetric Enigma: How Tall Was Matilda?', *Journal of Obstetrics and Gynaecology*, 1 (1981), pp. 271–2.

3. THE PLEDGE

1. *Anglo-Saxon Chronicle*, D, 1051.
2. Morris, *Norman Conquest*, pp. 11–19.
3. Ibid., pp. 19–22, 34–42.
4. Ibid., pp. 62–5, 68–72.
5. *Anglo-Saxon Chronicle*, D, 1051; *William of Poitiers*, pp. 18–21; *Gesta Normannorum Ducum*, vol. 2, pp. 158–9; S. Baxter, 'Edward the Confessor and the Succession Question', in *Edward the Confessor: The Man and the Legend*, ed. R. Mortimer (Woodbridge: Boydell, 2009), pp. 82–95; E. John, 'Edward the Confessor and the Norman Succession', *English Historical Review*, 94 (1979), pp. 241–67; Morris, *Norman Conquest*, pp. 64–5, 365.
6. Morris, *Norman Conquest*, pp. 19–20; *William of Poitiers*, pp. 18–21.
7. P. Grierson, 'The Relations Between England and Flanders Before the Norman Conquest', *Transactions of the Royal Historical Society*, 4th ser., 23 (1941), pp. 97–9.
8. John, 'Edward the Confessor', pp. 253–5.
9. Morris, *Norman Conquest*, pp. 75–9.

4. BAD NEIGHBOURS

1. Baxter, 'Edward the Confessor', pp. 90–91; William of Malmesbury, *Gesta Regum*, pp. 430–31; *William of Poitiers*, pp. 20–21, 50–51.
2. *William of Poitiers*, pp. 14–17.
3. *Gesta Normannorum Ducum*, vol. 2, pp. 122–5; *William of Poitiers*, pp. 22–9.
4. *William of Poitiers*, pp. 18–19, 44–5; D. Bates, *William the Conqueror* (London: George Philip, 1989), p. 35.
5. Douglas, *William the Conqueror*, pp. 40–41; *William of Poitiers*, pp. 32–9.
6. *William of Poitiers*, pp. 38–49; *Gesta Normannorum Ducum*, vol. 2, pp. 102–5.
7. *William of Poitiers*, pp. 18–19; J. Gillingham, 'William the Bastard at War', in *The Battle of Hastings: Sources and Interpretations*, ed. S. Morillo (Woodbridge: Boydell, 1996), pp. 99–107.
8. *Gesta Normannorum Ducum*, vol. 2, pp. 142–5; *William of Poitiers*, pp. 48–55.
9. Morris, *Norman Conquest*, pp. 85–6.
10. Ibid., pp. 93–4.
11. Ibid., pp. 110–11.
12. Ibid., pp. 86–93, 112.

5. EARL HAROLD

1. *Anglo-Saxon Chronicle*, C, 1053.
2. *The Life of King Edward who Rests at Westminster*, ed. F. Barlow (2nd edn, Oxford: Clarendon Press, 1992), pp. xxiii, 46–9; Baxter, 'Edward the Confessor', pp. 103–4.
3. *Life of King Edward*, pp. 48–9, 60–63; Morris, *Norman Conquest*, pp. 104–9.

4. Morris, *Norman Conquest*, pp. 101–3, 105–6.

5. *William of Poitiers*, pp. 68–9 (also *Gesta Normannorum Ducum*, vol. 2, pp. 158–61); William of Malmesbury, *Gesta Regum*, pp. 416–17.

6. *Eadmer's History of Recent Events in England*, ed. G. Bosanquet (London: Cresset Press, 1964), pp. 6–7; *William of Poitiers*, pp. 68–9; F. Barlow, *Edward the Confessor* (2nd edn, New Haven and London: Yale University Press, 1997), pp. 301–6; K. E. Cutler, 'The Godwinist Hostages: The Case for 1051', *Annuale Medievale*, 12 (1972), pp. 70–77.

7. *Eadmer's History*, p. 6.

8. *English Historical Documents, 1042–1189*, ed. D. C. Douglas and G. W. Greenaway (London: Eyre and Spottiswoode, 1953), pp. 239–46.

9. Ibid., pp. 247–52; *William of Poitiers*, pp. 70–79; *Eadmer's History*, pp. 6–8.

10. Morris, *Norman Conquest*, pp. 120–31.

6. THE ROAD TO HASTINGS

1. *William of Poitiers*, pp. 100–101; Morris, *Norman Conquest*, pp. 133–9.

2. Morris, *Norman Conquest*, pp. 142–3, 373; *William of Poitiers*, pp. 104–5.

3. Morris, *Norman Conquest*, pp. 143–6; *Gesta Normannorum Ducum*, vol. 2, pp. 162–3; *William of Poitiers*, pp. 140–43.

4. Morris, *Norman Conquest*, pp. 147–9; *Orderic Vitalis*, vol. 2, pp. 140–43; *Anglo-Saxon Chronicle*, C, 1066.

5. Morris, *Norman Conquest*, pp. 149–54, 166–8; *The Carmen de Hastingae Proelio of Guy, Bishop of Amiens*, ed. F. Barlow (Oxford: Clarendon Press, 1999), pp. 4–5.

6. *Carmen de Hastingae Proelio*, pp. 4–7; *Anglo-Saxon Chronicle*, C, 1066; *William of Poitiers*, pp. 108–11.

7. Morris, *Norman Conquest*, pp. 155–62.

8. *Carmen de Hastingae Proelio*, pp. 6–9; *William of Poitiers*, pp. 112–13.

9. Morris, *Norman Conquest*, pp. 164–5, 169–73.

10. Ibid., pp. 171–2, 174; *Anglo-Saxon Chronicle*, E, 1066; *William of Poitiers*, pp. 122–5.

11. *William of Poitiers*, pp. 122–5; *Gesta Normannorum Ducum*, pp. 168–9; *Anglo-Saxon Chronicle*, D, 1066.

12. *William of Poitiers*, pp. 124–5.

13. Morris, *Norman Conquest*, pp. 178–80.

14. *William of Poitiers*, pp. 128–9; *Carmen de Hastingae Proelio*, pp. 22–5.

15. *Carmen de Hastingae Proelio*, pp. 26–9; *William of Poitiers*, pp. 128–33.

16. Morris, *Norman Conquest*, pp. 183–8.

7. RESISTANCE

1. *William of Poitiers*, pp. 136–43; *Carmen de Hastingae Proelio*, pp. 36–7; *Anglo-Saxon Chronicle*, D, 1066.

2. *Anglo-Saxon Chronicle*, D, 1066; *William of Poitiers*, pp. 142–7; *Carmen de Hastingae Proelio*, pp. 36–9.

NOTES TO PAGES 52–70

3. Morris, *Norman Conquest*, pp. 193–8.
4. *William of Poitiers*, pp. 150–55, 178–9; Douglas, *Conqueror*, p. 209.
5. Morris, *Norman Conquest*, pp. 201–2.
6. *William of Poitiers*, pp. 162–3, 166–81; *Orderic Vitalis*, vol. 2, pp. 198–9.
7. *Orderic Vitalis*, vol. 2, pp. 202–3; *William of Poitiers*, pp. 180–83; *Anglo-Saxon Chronicle*, D, 1066.
8. Morris, *Norman Conquest*, pp. 209–22.
9. Ibid., pp. 215, 217, 221; *William of Poitiers*, pp. 156–7.
10. Morris, *Norman Conquest*, pp. 222–4.
11. Ibid., pp. 225–9.
12. Ibid., pp. 229–31; *Orderic Vitalis*, vol. 2, pp. 230–33; J. J. N. Palmer, 'War and Domesday Waste', *Armies, Chivalry and Warfare in Medieval Britain and France*, ed. M. Strickland (Stamford: Paul Watkins, 1998), pp. 256–75.
13. Morris, *Norman Conquest*, pp. 232–40, 242–5.
14. Ibid., pp. 243–4, 246–50; *Orderic Vitalis*, vol. 2, pp. 256–9.

8. ENEMIES FOREIGN AND DOMESTIC

1. *Orderic Vitalis*, vol. 2, pp. 258–61.
2. Simeon of Durham, *History of the Kings of England*, trans. J. Stevenson (facsimile reprint, Lampeter: Llanerch Press, 1987), pp. 138–40; *Anglo-Saxon Chronicle*, E, 1072; *The Chronicle of John of Worcester*, ed. R. R. Darlington and P. McGurk, trans. J. Bray and P. McGurk, vol. 3 (Oxford: Clarendon Press, 1998), pp. 20–21.
3. Douglas, *William the Conqueror*, pp. 212, 224–5.
4. Ibid., pp. 223–4, 228–9.
5. *Anglo-Saxon Chronicle*, D and E, 1073; *Anglo-Saxon Chronicle*, D, 1074.
6. Morris, *Norman Conquest*, pp. 267–70; *The Letters of Lanfranc, Archbishop of Canterbury*, ed. and trans. V. H. Clover and M. Gibson (Oxford: Clarendon Press, 1979), pp. 124–5.
7. Morris, *Norman Conquest*, pp. 253, 268, 270–71; *Orderic Vitalis*, vol. 2, pp. 314–15, 318–23.
8. *Orderic Vitalis*, vol. 2, pp. 350–53; Douglas, *William the Conqueror*, pp. 230–34; *Anglo-Saxon Chronicle*, D and E, 1076.
9. Morris, *Norman Conquest*, pp. 273–6, 288.
10. *Orderic Vitalis*, vol. 3, pp. 102–5; *Minor Latin Poets*, vol. 2, trans. J. Wight Duff and A. M. Duff (Loeb Classical Library 434, Cambridge, MA: Harvard University Press, 1934), pp. 624–5.
11. *Orderic Vitalis*, vol. 3, pp. 110–13; Bates, *William the Conqueror*, p. 163.
12. *Orderic Vitalis*, vol. 2, pp. 264–5; Morris, *Norman Conquest*, p. 290.
13. Morris, *Norman Conquest*, pp. 291–4.
14. *Anglo-Saxon Chronicle*, E, 1081; D. A. E. Pelteret, *Slavery in Early Mediaeval England* (Woodbridge: Boydell, 1995), *passim*; D. Wyatt, *Slaves and Warriors in Medieval Britain and Ireland, 800–1200* (Leiden: Brill, 2009), *passim*; Morris, *Norman Conquest*, pp. 294–6; J. Gillingham, *The English in the Twelfth Century* (Woodbridge: Boydell, 2000), pp. xvii–xviii.
15. E. Fernie, *The Architecture of Norman England* (Oxford: Clarendon Press, 2000), pp. 55–67, 102–3, 117–21; *Orderic Vitalis*, vol. 3, pp. 232–3.

16. *Orderic Vitalis*, vol. 2, pp. 264–5; Morris, *Norman Conquest*, pp. 300–302.

17. Morris, *Norman Conquest*, pp. 302–4; *Orderic Vitalis*, vol. 4, pp. 78–9.

9. DOMESDAY

1. *Anglo-Saxon Chronicle*, E, 1085; William of Malmesbury, *Gesta Regum*, pp. 474–5, 480–81; E. M. C. van Houts, 'The Norman Conquest Through European Eyes', *English Historical Review*, 110 (1995), pp. 837–8.

2. William of Malmesbury, *Saints' Lives*, ed. M. Winterbottom and R. M. Thomson (Oxford: Clarendon Press, 2002), pp. 130–31; J. R. Maddicott, 'Responses to the Threat of Invasion, 1085', *English Historical Review*, 122 (2007), pp. 986–97; *Anglo-Saxon Chronicle*, E, 1085.

3. S. Baxter, 'Domesday Book', *BBC History Magazine*, 11 (August 2010), p. 24; *English Historical Documents*, p. 530.

4. Morris, *Norman Conquest*, pp. 308–11.

5. Ibid., pp. 291, 312–18.

6. J. C. Holt, '1086', in *Domesday Studies*, ed. idem (Woodbridge: Boydell, 1987), pp. 41–64; *Anglo-Saxon Chronicle*, E, 1086.

7. Morris, *Norman Conquest*, pp. 322–5; G. Garnett, *Conquered England: Kingship, Succession and Tenure, 1066–1166* (Oxford: Clarendon Press, 2007), p. 345.

8. *Anglo-Saxon Chronicle*, E, 1086; *English Historical Documents*, p. 851; Morris, *Norman Conquest*, pp. 325–6.

10. CONCLUSION

1. William of Malmesbury, *Gesta Regum*, pp. 510–11; *Orderic Vitalis*, vol. 4, pp. 78–81, 92–101; B. English, 'William the Conqueror and the Anglo-Norman Succession', *Historical Research*, 64 (1991), pp. 221–36.

2. *Orderic Vitalis*, vol. 4, pp. 100–107.

3. Ibid., pp. 78–9, 106–9; Van Houts, 'Norman Conquest Through European Eyes', pp. 851–2.

4. Other obituaries of William are not so accurate. *De Obitu Willelmi* (translated in *English Historical Documents*, pp. 279–80) was assembled from ninth-century obituaries of Charlemagne and Louis the Pious. K. Lack, 'The *De Obitu Willelmi*: Propaganda for the Anglo-Norman Succession, 1087–88?', *English Historical Review*, 123 (2008), pp. 1417–56.

   A passage of Hugh of Flavigny's chronicle often said to describe William as affable, generous and eloquent is actually a description of Richard, Abbot of Verdun (d. 1046). This error probably originates from a misreading of R. W. Southern, *The Making of the Middle Ages* (London: Hutchinson, 1953), p. 152. Cf. Douglas, *William the Conqueror*, pp. 375–6 and Bates, *William the Conqueror*, p. 94.

5. *Anglo-Saxon Chronicle*, E, 1087. The author betrays no knowledge of Henry I's accession in 1100.

6. Ibid.; H. G. Richardson and G. O. Sayles, *Law and Legislation from Æthelbert to Magna Carta* (Edinburgh: Edinburgh University Press, 1966), pp. 10, 16, 20–21.

NOTES TO PAGES 84–88

7. Bates, *William the Conqueror*, p. 93; Guibert of Nogent, *Monodies and On the Relics of Saints*, trans. J. McAlhany and J. Rubenstein (London: Penguin, 2011), p. 36; Morris, *Norman Conquest*, p. 329.

8. J. Gillingham, '1066 and the Introduction of Chivalry into England', *Law and Government in Medieval England and Normandy*, ed. G. Garnett and J. Hudson (Cambridge: Cambridge University Press, 1994), pp. 31–55.

9. William of Malmesbury, *Gesta Regum*, pp. 492–3, 496–9; *English Historical Documents*, p. 647.

10. William of Malmesbury, *Gesta Regum*, pp. 500–503.

11. E. A. Freeman, *The History of the Norman Conquest of England*, vol. 2 (2nd edn, rev., Oxford: Clarendon Press, 1870), pp. 608–10; M. de Boüard 'Note sur l'appellation "Guillaume le Conquérant"', *Studies in Medieval History Presented to R. Allen Brown*, ed. C. Harper-Bill, C. J. Holdsworth and J. L. Nelson (Woodbridge: Boydell, 1989), pp. 21–6; J. Gillingham, '"Slaves of the Normans?": Gerald de Barri and Regnal Solidarity in Early Thirteenth-Century England', *Law, Laity and Solidarities: Essays in Honour of Susan Reynolds*, ed. P. Stafford, J. L. Nelson and J. Martindale (Manchester: Manchester University Press, 2001), p. 170; *Anglo-Saxon Chronicle*, D, 1066.

12. D. Bates, 'The Conqueror's Earliest Historians and the Writing of his Biography', *Writing Medieval Biography 750–1250: Essays in Honour of Professor Frank Barlow*, ed. D. Bates, J. Crick and S. Hamilton (Woodbridge: Boydell, 2006), pp. 129–41; *English Historical Documents*, pp. 606–7.

13. *Orderic Vitalis*, vol. 2, pp. 234–7; *Anglo-Saxon Chronicle*, E, 1087.

Further Reading

William I still awaits a full-scale modern biography. The last such study was D. C. Douglas, *William the Conqueror: The Norman Impact Upon England* (London: Methuen, 1964) which, although dated in places, can still be read with profit. D. Bates, *William the Conqueror* (London: George Philip, 1989) is livelier and a little more up to date but lacks academic references.

Shorter but incisive accounts of William's career can be found in D. Carpenter, *The Struggle for Mastery: Britain, 1066–1284* (London: Allen Lane, 2003) and M. T. Clanchy, *England and Its Rulers, 1066–1272* (4th edition, Oxford: Wiley-Blackwell, 2014).

The early history of Normandy is covered in D. Bates, *Normandy Before 1066* (London: Longman, 1982) and D. Crouch, *The Normans* (London: Hambledon, 2002), while William's own early years are dealt with in D. Bates, 'The Conqueror's Adolescence', *Anglo-Norman Studies*, vol. 25 (2003). William's military methods are analysed in J. Gillingham, 'William the Bastard at War', *Studies in Medieval History Presented to R. A. Brown*, edited by C. Harper-Bill, C. Holdsworth and J. Nelson (Woodbridge: Boydell, 1989), and his political methods in J. Gillingham, '1066 and the Introduction of Chivalry into England', in idem, *The English in the Twelfth Century: Imperialism, National Identity and Political Values* (Woodbridge: Boydell, 2000).

For England before the Conquest, F. Barlow, *Edward the Confessor* (2nd edition, New Haven and London: Yale University Press, 1997) remains the standard biography, though in places its conclusions are perverse, and need to be tempered with the essays in *Edward the Confessor: The Man and the Legend*, edited by R. Mortimer (Woodbridge: Boydell, 2009), especially S. Baxter, 'Edward the Confessor and the Succession Question'. For pre-Conquest England in general, *The Anglo-Saxons*, edited by J. Campbell (London: Penguin, 1991), remains a scholarly, solid and lavishly illustrated introduction.

For the Conquest in general, see M. Morris, *The Norman Conquest* (London: Hutchinson, 2012) and H. M. Thomas, *The Norman Conquest: England After William the Conqueror* (Lanham: Rowman and Littlefield, 2008). G. Garnett, *The Norman Conquest: A Very Short Introduction* (Oxford: Oxford University Press, 2009) is an accessible primer for the more complicated arguments set out in the same author's *Conquered England: Kingship, Succession and Tenure, 1066–1166* (Oxford: Oxford University Press, 2007).

M. K. Lawson, *The Battle of Hastings* (Stroud: Tempus, 2002) provides the best analysis of the battle itself, although its estimations of the troop numbers need to treated with caution.

For the rebuilding of England after 1066, see E. Fernie, *The Architecture of Norman England* (Oxford: Oxford University Press, 2000).

Happily all the major primary sources for William's career are now available in English translation. The most important are *The Gesta Guillelmi of William of Poitiers*, edited by R. H. C. Davis and M. Chibnall (Oxford: Clarendon Press, 1998), *The Ecclesiastical History of Orderic Vitalis*, edited by M. Chibnall (6 vols, Oxford: Clarendon Press, 1968–80), and *The Anglo-Saxon Chronicle*, edited by G. N. Garmonsway (2nd edition, London: Everyman, 1972). Excerpts from these writers and a wealth of other primary source material can be found in *English Historical Documents, 1042–1189*, edited by D. C. Douglas and G. W. Greenaway (London: Eyre and Spottiswoode, 1953).

Picture Credits

1. William as Duke of Normandy, Bayeux Tapestry, late eleventh century (akg-images/Erich Lessing)
2. Harold Godwineson approaches Edward the Confessor, Bayeux Tapestry, late eleventh century (akg-images/Erich Lessing)
3. Bishop Odo of Bayeux at the Battle of Hastings, Bayeux Tapestry, late eleventh century (akg-images/IAM)
4. The early Norman castle at York, reconstruction (© Historic England)
5. The Normans building a castle at Hastings, Bayeux Tapestry, late eleventh century (Musée de la Tapisserie, Bayeux, France/Bridgeman Images)
6. St John's Chapel, Tower of London (© Hemis/Alamy Stock Photo)
7. The Norman great tower at Chepstow Castle
8. Men ploughing the land, Anglo-Saxon calendar, eleventh century. Cotton Tiberius B. V, Part 1, f.3 (© The British Library Board)
9. Obverse of a silver penny from the reign of William I (Fitzwilliam Museum, University of Cambridge, UK/Bridgeman Images)
10. A page from the Yorkshire section of the Domesday Book (Mary Evans/The National Archives, London)
11. William the Conqueror on the throne, in the *Chronicle of Battle Abbey*. Ms. Cotton Domitian A.II, fol. 22. London, British Library (akg-images/British Library)
12. St Étienne, Caen, nave interior (© John Elk III/Alamy Stock Photo)

Acknowledgements

I am very grateful to David D'Avray for translating a long section of Hugh of Flavigny's chronicle, and proving that what is often taken as a complimentary description of William I is in fact an encomium for Abbot Richard of Verdun. My thanks to Colin Veach for sending me a scan of Ralph Glaber's comments on William's birth, and to Tom Penn, Anna Hervé, Linden Lawson and all their colleagues at Penguin who helped get the book to press.

Index